Monograph #13

World Court Enhancements to Advance The Rule of Law

By Bryan F. MacPherson

Published By
The Center for U.N. Reform Education
139 East McClellan Avenue
Livingston, NJ 07039
(201) 994-1826

June, 1994

ISBN 1-881520-03-X

About the Center

The Center for U.N. Reform Education was formed in 1978 following a conference on U.N. reform at Villanova University. Subsequent conferences were held at the University of Chicago, New York University, University of Bridgeport, Kaiser Conference Center in Oakland, California, and in Los Angeles near the University of Southern California.

Since 1987 the Center has concentrated on publishing a series of carefully researched monographs on ways to improve the U.N. system. The firs twelve are listed on the back cover. A 15 member Board of Trustees, elected by the 25 organizations affiliated with the Center review and approve each monograph before it is published. The affiliated organizations are listed on the next page.

The Center, a non-profit educational organization, does not take positions regarding any particular U.N. reform proposal, but encourages wide discussion. Contributions to the Center are tax deductible.

* * * * * * * * * *

Officers of the Center for U.N. Reform Education

Affiliated Organizations

of the

CENTER FOR U.N. REFORM EDUCATION

Participating Organizations

B'nai B'rith International
Campaign for U.N. Reform
Center for War/Peace Studies
Global Education Association
World Federalist Association

Cooperating Organizations

American Jewish Congress
Americans for Democratic Action
B'nai B'rith Women
California-Nevada Annual Conference of the United Methodist Church
Campaign for a More Democratic United Nations
Center for the Development of International Law
Clergy and Laity Concerned
Common Heritage Institute
Consortium of Peace Research, Education and Development
Fellowship of Reconciliation
Friends Committee on National Legislation
International Public Policy Institute
International Studies Association
Northern California Ecumenical Council
Pace Peace Center
Women of Reform Judaism
World Order Models Project
World Policy Institute
World Without War Council

The Center welcomes other organizations that may wish to affiliate with it as either a Participation or Cooperating Organization.

Abstract

World Court Enhancements to Advance The Rule of Law, by Bryan F. MacPherson (June 1994) (C.U.R.E. Monograph #13). 78 pages.

Adherence to the rule of law in relations among states would benefit all nations by increasing the prospect for world peace and justice. Where law is absent, anarchy reigns and the world is governed by might, not by right. The expectations of many that creation of the International Court of Justice (ICJ) would solve most of the problems of compliance with international law and would ensure peace have not been fulfilled. No court alone, absent other organs of government including a method of legislating new laws and a method of ensuring compliance with court judgments, can have any hope of ensuring the rule of law. The Court is also hampered because its jurisdiction is based upon the consent of the states concerned; consequently, it cannot compel states to appear. Nonetheless, the ICJ can play an important role in the peaceful and just resolution of disputes. While the Court has had some successes, it has not lived up to its potential and remains seriously underutilized by the world community.

This monograph describes the operation of the Court, and explains how an effective Court could contribute to world peace and justice. The paper examines the reasons why the ICJ has been underutilized, and it recommends measures that will allow the Court to play a more significant role in the future. The monograph also discusses measures that the U.S. should take to demonstrate its support for the Court and the rule of law. Some of the paper's principal recommendations are:

- States must change their attitude to recognize that even though they may occasionally lose a case, in the long run everyone benefits from the rule of law. States should make a commitment to the rule of law and demonstrate this commitment by bringing disputes before the Court. States should signify their commitment by (1) including compromissory clauses in treaties, (2) entering into a general dispute resolution convention that provides for ICJ resolution, and (3) accepting the Court's general jurisdiction under the optional clause. The U.S. should exercise leadership in this regard. It should, for example, emphasize its commitment to the rule of law by filing a new declaration that does not contain debilitating reservations such as the Connally reservation.
- Nations must be confident that the Court will fairly and effectively decide the cases before it. The ICJ can itself institute some changes to encourage use of the Court. It should, for example, improve its evidence gathering capabilities, reconsider the weight to be given various types of evidence, and be more receptive to intervention requests. The ICJ should amend its rules to allow non-state parties whose interests are at stake to participate in ICJ proceedings to a greater extent.
- Organizations should be encouraged to make greater use of the ICJ's advisory jurisdiction. The General Assembly should authorize the Secretary General, as well as additional organizations, to request advisory opinions. The Statute might also be amended so that all U.N. organs and agencies can obtain advisory opinions without first being authorized by the General Assembly.
- The General Assembly should establish a screening committee with authority to request advisory opinions upon the request of national courts or organizations outside of the U.N. system, including possibly non-governmental organizations. The screening committee should be a non-political body, and to ensure that it does not screen out possibly meritorious cases, a specified minority of the members, e.g., 30 to 40 percent, should be sufficient to request an opinion.
- The Security Council must place a greater priority on the enforcement of ICJ judgments, and a convention should be drafted that would require states to enforce judgments. Even in the absence of such a convention, however, nations, including the U.S., should amend their domestic laws to facilitate enforcement of ICJ judgments.
- International organizations should be permitted to appear as parties to contentious cases. This would, for example, allow the Court to exercise some degree of judicial review over the legality of an organization's activities. Consideration should be given to amending the Statute to provide for compulsory jurisdiction in inter-state disputes. Only through compulsory jurisdiction would states, especially smaller states, be guaranteed that they can vindicate their rights through the judicial process.

CONTENTS

PREFACE

The term "World Court" is commonly applied by the media to the International Court of Justice, which the U.N. Charter has designated as "the principal judicial organ of the United Nations." The term "International Court" more accurately defines the present court because, with the exception of advisory opinions, it only hears cases that are brought by one nation-state against another.

Nevertheless, both the Center for U.N. Reform Education and Bryan MacPherson, the author of this monograph, prefer the term "World Court," not only because of its common usage by the media, but also because it symbolizes the hopes of many that the present international court will evolve and develop into a true world court that will some day apply globally recognized and codified standards of world law to individuals and organizations as well as nation-states.

If the international court that sits at the Hague today is to evolve into a genuine world court, its Statute, rules, procedures, and methods of enforcement will have to be strengthened. Mr. MacPherson has, in a scholarly fashion, suggested a number of specific ways to enhance the work and authority of the Court. His goal is the promotion of the rule of law, the key to achieving a more peaceful and just world.

Readers of the Center's monographs will recall that Mr. MacPherson was the author of Monograph #10, entitled "An International Criminal Court: Applying World Law to Individuals." His bold proposals in that monograph were circulated to both the U.S. Departments of State and Justice, to several key missions at the United Nations, and to all members of the International Law Commission prior to their own preparation of a draft statute for an International Criminal Court. That draft statute was discussed by the General Assembly last fall.

Mr. MacPherson, a member of the Washington D.C. Bar, has worked for 15 years in the Office of Hearings and Appeals of the U.S. Department of Energy. He holds no less than four degrees: a B.S. from Oregon State University, an M.S. from the University of Illinois, a J.D. from the Washington College of Law of the American University, and an LL.M. from the London School of Economics, where he concentrated his studies in the areas of criminal and international law.

The views expressed in this monograph, as in all monographs of the Center, are those of the author alone and do not necessarily reflect the policies or ideas of the Center or any of its affiliated organizations, nor do they reflect the views of the Department of Energy.

Comments on this monograph and requests for copies of some of the documents cited would be most welcome.

Walter Hoffmann
President
Center for U.N. Reform Education

I. INTRODUCTION

Throughout history societies have employed numerous methods to maintain order and to resolve the disputes that invariably arise. The quality of dispute resolution has varied greatly. Law and justice could be arbitrary. It often was based upon the whim of the ruler, and not every ruler had the wisdom of Solomon. Many methods of dispute resolution have been based upon superstition, such as trial by combat or by ordeal.[1] On the other hand, the Athenian legal system in the 6th century B.C.E., included a system of trial by jury. While there are exceptions, most modern nations are governed by the rule of law, i.e., by systems of laws that carefully specify in advance each person's rights and duties with respect to other individuals and to the state. The cornerstone of most modern legal systems is an impartial judicial system that resolves disputes by determining the relevant facts and applying the law to these facts.

> [T]he rule of law must somehow be established to provide a way of settling disputes among nations as it does among individuals. . . . [T]he rule of law must replace the balance of terror as the paramount factor in the affairs of men. . . . [The United States] should be prepared to show the world by our example that the rule of law, even in the most trying of circumstances, is the one system which all free men of good will must support.
>
> *Vice President Richard Nixon*
> *Address to the Academy of Political Science (April 13, 1959)*

The rule of law is equally important at the international level. An equitable system of law can promote peace and justice. Where law is absent, anarchy reigns and the world is governed by might, not by right. The development and growth of international law over the last two centuries has been a major step toward the establishment of the rule of law for the world community. But, international law is still in its infancy—many aspects of international relations are not subject to clear rules of conduct, and there is no established method for legislating new international laws. A major weakness of the international legal system is the lack of a consistently effective method for enforcing those international laws that do exist; accordingly, many nations ignore international law when they believe it is in their interest to do so.

The International Court of Justice (ICJ) and its predecessor the Permanent Court of International Justice (PCIJ), which are commonly called the "World Court," were intended to play a central role in resolving disputes between states[2] on the basis of international law. It was thought that the World Court would play a role comparable to that of courts in national legal systems. Although the Court has had its successes, it has not lived up to these expectations. The Court has received little respect and has been severely underutilized by the world community. Even in those instances where the Court has been utilized, its decisions have too often been ignored. The Court's standing in the United States reached its nadir in 1985 when the U.S. withdrew its declaration accepting the general jurisdiction of the Court as

---

1/ Trial by combat and trial by ordeal are essentially calls for divine intervention to resolve the dispute.

2/ The terms "states" and "nations" are used throughout this monograph to mean sovereign national governments, not in the case of "states" to mean one of the 50 U.S. states, or in the case of "nations" to mean an ethnic group such as the "Cherokee nation."

a result of the case initiated by Nicaragua in 1984 over U.S. mining of Nicaraguan harbors and support of the Contra rebels. Prospects are looking up however. In the last few years, the ICJ has been busier than ever before in its history. There are currently nine contentious cases and one request for an advisory opinion on the Court's docket. While this is an encouraging trend, the ICJ's potential is much greater. Furthermore, the Court still does not appear to have the full confidence of the major powers. None of the cases pending before the Court were, for example, initiated by a permanent member of the Security Council.

The General Assembly has designated the 1990's to be the Decade of International Law. It is appropriate therefore that we examine the role that the ICJ, the U.N.'s principal judicial organ, plays in the international legal order and how that role might be enhanced. The purpose of this monograph is to describe the operation of the Court and how an effective Court could contribute to world peace and justice. This paper will examine the reasons why the ICJ has been largely underutilized and ineffective, and it will recommend measures that will allow the Court to play a more significant role in the world community. This paper will also discuss specific measures that the U.S. should take to demonstrate its support for the Court and the rule of law that are consistent with aspirations and interests of the United States.

> The docket of the International Court of Justice has grown fuller but it remains an under-used resource for the peaceful adjudication of disputes. Greater reliance on the Court would be an important contribution to United Nations peacemaking. . . . All member states should accept the general jurisdiction of the International Court . . . without reservation, before the end of the United Nations Decade of International Law in the year 2000.
>
> *Secretary-General Boutros-Ghali*
> *An Agenda for Peace—Preventive Diplomacy, Peacemaking, & Peacekeeping (1992)*

II. BACKGROUND

A. Methods of Dispute Settlement

Too often nations resort to force in order to resolve conflicts. Too much of our history books are devoted to tales of war and conquest. However, war is expensive, both in terms of lives and resources, so that even victory may not be worth the cost. Enlightened people throughout history have sought peaceful methods of resolving international disputes. Adjudication before the World Court is only one of these methods. The role of the World Court is best viewed in the context of other methods of dispute resolution. Dispute resolution mechanisms may be roughly grouped into two categories, diplomatic methods and adjudicatory methods. In addition to direct one-on-one negotiation, diplomatic methods include several by which third parties may assist in reaching a negotiated settlement. These assisted methods include good offices, mediation, enquiry, and conciliation. Adjudicatory methods include arbitration and judicial settlement. Article 33 of the U.N. Charter imposes the obligation upon member states to seek to resolve by peaceful means any dispute that may threaten international peace and security. The principal methods of resolving international disputes peacefully are summarized below:[3]

1. Negotiation: Negotiation, the process by which nations bargain directly with each other is the predominate method of resolving international disputes. Negotiation gives the parties the most control over the process, and it is usually the most effective method of settling international disputes. It is efficient since it does not involve the intervention of outside parties, and states are more likely to accept settlements reached by consent than they are to accept settlements imposed upon them. Most disputes are settled through direct negotiations.

2. Good Offices: When direct negotiations are not successful, there are several methods by which third parties—other states, individuals, or international organizations—can assist the parties to reach a negotiated settlement. When the parties to a dispute refuse even to talk to each other, a third party may offer its good offices. Good offices consists of bringing the parties to the negotiating table.

3. Mediation: In mediation, a third party actively assists the parties to reach an acceptable negotiated settlement. The mediator may advise the parties and suggest possible settlements. Mediation is generally somewhat informal and confidential.

4. Enquiry: Where a dispute involves questions of fact, the parties may agree to have a commission of enquiry or a fact-finding mission attempt to resolve the factual issues. The report of a commission of enquiry is generally limited to a statement of the factual findings. The effect to be given the report is up to the parties. Nonetheless, an unbiased investigation of the relevant facts may form a basis for a negotiated settlement.

3/ For a more complete discussion of international dispute settlement mechanisms see R. Bilder, *An Overview of International Dispute Settlement*, 1 J. OF INT'L DISPUTE RESOLUTION 1 (1986); L. Sohn, *The Future of Dispute Settlement* in THE STRUCTURE & PROCESS OF INTERNATIONAL LAW: ESSAYS IN LEGAL PHILOSOPHY, DOCTRINE & THEORY 1121 (R. Macdonald & D. Johnston eds. 1986).

5. Conciliation: Conciliation is often combined with enquiry. A conciliation commission usually presents to the parties a proposed resolution that it believes most appropriate and asks them to respond to it. It then issues a final report. If a settlement is reached, the report consists of the terms of the settlement, and if no settlement is obtained, the report consists of a summary of the work and recommendations of the commission.

6. Arbitration: Unlike the methods of assisting negotiations listed above, both arbitration and judicial adjudications lead to determinations that are nominally binding upon the parties. The structure of the arbitral panel and the manner in which the arbitration is conducted is by agreement of the parties. This agreement may be expressed either in a pre-existing treaty or in a special agreement (*compromis*) prepared for the specific arbitration. The agreement will specify the makeup of the arbitral panel or the manner in which it is to be selected. It may also specify the law to be applied, for example, it may exclude application of a rule of international law that is not accepted by one of the parties. Alternatively, the *compromis* may provide, especially where there is no applicable rule of law, that the decision will be decided *ex aequo et bono* (an equitable settlement made, if necessary, in disregard of existing law). Arbitrations may be conducted by a single individual—heads of state, the Pope, distinguished jurists and diplomats have all served as sole arbitrators. More common today are arbitrations conducted by a panel of arbitrators. There are two principal types. Mixed claims commissions usually have two national members who attempt to reach an agreement and an umpire to whom the cases are referred if the national members cannot agree. Ordinary arbitral tribunals, however, generally consist of three or five members who decide cases by a majority vote. Generally the members are chosen by common agreement or each party selects one or two of the members with the remaining member(s) chosen by agreement or through an agreed upon mechanism.[4]

7. Judicial Determinations: Judicial determinations constitute the most formal method of resolving international disputes. Besides the World Court, there are a number of other international courts. These include the Court of Justice of the European Communities, the Benlux Court of Justice, the European Court of Human Rights, and the Inter-American Court of Human Rights. Unlike the ICJ, some of these courts allow individuals to appear as parties. Courts differ from arbitral panels in that they are standing permanent tribunals with set rules of procedure that base their decisions upon international law, while arbitral panels are usually created *ad hoc*, and the agreement setting up the panel specifies the rules of procedure and the law that will be applied. Judicial decisions are more likely than arbitral awards to constitute precedents for deciding future cases.

8. Regional & International Organizations: Nations may also seek the assistance of the U.N., its associated agencies, regional organizations (such as the Organization of American States (OAS) or the Organization for African Unity (OAU)) or other international organizations as a means of settling disputes. The Secretary General is often called upon to help mediate disputes and the General Assembly (Article 11) may assist in dispute resolution by passing non-binding resolutions. The Security Council, of course, plays a pivotal role in dispute settlement. Under Chapter VI of the Charter, it may recommend procedures for the settlement of disputes that are likely to endanger international peace, and may with the consent of the parties make specific recommendations as to settlement. Under Chapter VII,

---

4/ For a more detailed explanation of international arbitration see J. BARATTA, INTERNATIONAL ARBITRATION: IMPROVING ITS ROLE IN DISPUTE SETTLEMENT (1989) (Monograph #7 published by the Center for U.N. Reform Education).

the Security Council may make decisions, binding on all members of the U.N., to impose a settlement in cases involving a threat to peace, breach of peace or act of aggression. Regional and international organizations may utilize any of the methods described above or may utilize other methods as mechanisms for dispute settlement. The Contadora process, which resolved much of the conflict in Central America, is an example of a successful regional intervention.

The foregoing methods of settling international disputes do not exhaust the possibilities of peaceful settlement, nor are there sharp boundaries among them.[5] Various methods of resolution may be employed in *seriatim*. For example, President Carter's role in the Camp David Accords which settled many of the differences between Egypt and Israel included both that of providing good offices and that of mediator. It should be noted that most of the methods of settling international disputes may be used, in modified form, to resolve disputes between individuals.

B. Historical Background

1. Growth of Arbitration

Greek city-states included arbitration as one of several mechanisms for resolving disputes among them. Arbitration was used on an irregular basis in Europe throughout the Middle Ages, although in many cases the arbitrators acted more as mediators or conciliators. Often, heads of state were called upon to be arbitrators, and the Pope was a frequent choice. His role as the head of the common religion of the age increased the prestige of his decisions and the probability that they would be obeyed. However, the Pope was not acceptable in all cases. Sovereigns who were out of favor with the Pope might fear a biased decision, and increased Papal authority meant lessened authority for national sovereigns. The Pope's utility as an arbitrator waned as the Reformation destroyed the religious unity of the continent.[6]

The rate of arbitrations increased substantially during the 19th Century. According to one study:

- From 1789 to 1840 there were 23 international arbitrations (1 every 2 years).
- From 1841 to 1860 there were 20 (1 per year).
- From 1861 to 1880 there were 44 (2 per year).
- From 1881 to 1900 there were 90 (4½ per year).[7]

More important than the increase in the number of cases was the evolution in the manner in which the cases were submitted to arbitration. Traditionally, arbitrations had been initiated

---

5/ In March 1994, the Special Committee on Review of the U.N. Charter had before it a working paper, submitted by Sierra Leone, which called for establishment of a U.N. Dispute Settlement Service.

6/ A. BUSTAMANTE, THE WORLD COURT, ¶¶ 5-6 (1925). The Pope still is occasionally called upon to help resolve international disputes. In 1980 he mediated the Beagle Channel dispute between Argentina and Chile. 24 I.L.M. 1, 7 (1985).

7/ BUSTAMANTE, *supra* note 6, at ¶ 7.

by a *compromis,* a special agreement between the parties to submit a specific conflict to arbitration. The 19th Century saw the insertion into treaties of compromissory clauses that provided in advance for the arbitration of disputes involving matters related to that treaty. Finally, general arbitration treaties were developed that provided for arbitration of any differences, within specified parameters, that might arise between the parties.[8]

2. Early Court Proposals

Perhaps the first concrete proposal for a standing court to resolve international disputes was made early in the 14th century by the French jurist Pierre Dubois. The primary purpose of his proposal, and many that followed it, was to ensure peace among the Christian nations of the world so that they might more effectively battle the "infidels."[9] Near the end of the 17th Century, William Penn proposed a permanent Diet where each nation would be represented in proportion to its economic power. Disputes that could not be resolved through diplomatic means were to be submitted to the Diet. A section of ten of its members would constitute a court. If a state refused to submit a dispute to the Diet or to carry out a decision of the court all other rulers were to unite their forces to compel it to comply.[10] This is remarkably similar to the obligation of member-states of the U.N. to submit unresolved disputes to the Security Council pursuant to Article 37 of the Charter and to the obligation of members, under Articles 25, 48 and 49, to carry out enforcement decisions of the Security Council.

Jeremy Bentham developed a plan for international peace toward the end of the 18th century that included a court. He noted that "The maintenance of stable peace could be greatly facilitated by the organization of a joint court of justice for the settlement of differences between nations even though the court could not exercise any coercive power."[11] John Stuart Mill, in discussing the requirements of a federal form of world government said "The supreme court of the federation will render decisions on questions of international law. This is the first instance of what is really one of the greatest necessities of civilized society, a genuine international court."[12] The last part of the 19th century through World War I saw an avalanche of proposals for a world court from individuals, international organizations and conferences. Organizations endorsing the idea of a world court included the General Peace Convention, International Law Association, the Interparliamentary Union, and the Institute of International Law.[13] Americans were members and participants in many of these organizations. In addition, a number of primarily American organizations also supported the idea including the American Society of International Law, the American Institute of International

8/ *Id.* ¶ 8.

9/ *Id* ¶ 9.

10/ *Id.* ¶ 11 (W. Penn, Essay on the Peace of Europe (1693). The Abbé de Saint-Pierre offered a similar proposal. *Id.* ¶ 12.

11/ *Id.* ¶ 13 (citing J. Bentham, Principles of International Law).

12/ *Id.* ¶ 14 (J.S. Mill, Considerations on Representative Government (1861)).

13/ *Id.* ¶¶ 17—50.

Law, the American Society for the Judicial Settlement of International Disputes, the Lake Mohonk Conference, and the New York State Bar Association.[14]

3. Hague Peace Conferences

In 1899 Russian Emperor Nicholas II convened a peace conference whose primary purpose was to consider disarmament as a method of ensuring peace. The 26 mostly European nations invited to attend recognized, however, that disarmament would not be possible without removing the fundamental reasons for armaments, and the conference was expanded to include the laws of war and methods for the settlement of disputes. Three conventions resulted from the first Hague conference. Two dealt with the laws of war. The third, which is of interest here, was the Convention for the Pacific Settlement of International Disputes.

The Hague Convention was unsatisfactorily weak. The international community was unwilling to surrender any control over dispute settlement to third parties. Nevertheless, it did affirm the desirability of peaceful settlement of disputes. The parties agreed to use their best efforts to ensure peaceful settlement of disputes and to have recourse, "as far as circumstances allow," to mediation, good offices, or commissions of inquiry. The convention also encouraged arbitration and created the "Permanent Court of Arbitration." This was a misnomer because it was neither permanent nor a court. The "Court" is a list of individuals (up to four from each nation) from which arbitrators can be selected by states wishing to arbitrate disputes. The convention also set forth the procedures to be used by the court in conducting arbitrations. The world was not yet ready to adopt proposals, including one advanced by the U.S., for a true international court. Nor was serious consideration given to proposals to make arbitration of disputes obligatory, although Article 19 of the Convention gave lip service to this idea by recognizing that states may conclude treaties requiring arbitration under specified circumstances. The Permanent Court of Arbitration has not been a major success—since its inception it has decided only a handful of cases. Today, its primary function is the nomination of ICJ judicial candidates.

Forty-four nations, nearly all of the world's independent countries at the time, were represented in 1907 at the second Hague Conference. The conference addressed in significant detail the twin questions of mandatory adjudication and creation of a true international court. The U.S. delegation under the direction of Secretary of State Elihu Root urged positive action on both of these issues.

Nations differed substantially on whether arbitration should be compulsory. Only two nations, Denmark and the Dominican Republic, were prepared to submit all disputes, without exception, to binding arbitration. Opposition to mandatory arbitration was led by Germany, which along with Austria, Belgium, and Greece, appeared unwilling to accept mandatory arbitration under any circumstances. Some nations were willing to accept compulsory arbitration over some classes of disputes, but not over others. The U.S. position favoring compulsory arbitration in principle was undermined to a large extent by the U.S. insistence that there be exceptions for matters involving "vital interests, independence and honor" or which were "purely American questions." In the end, the conference, while recognizing the desirability of compulsory adjudication, was unable to agree to any concrete proposals.

14/ *Id.* ¶¶ 29—37.

There was greater sentiment in favor of establishing a truly international court. The U.S. proposal called for a court that would have jurisdiction over disputes of an international nature between sovereign states which the parties agree to submit to the court. The court could be composed of 15 judges, appointed for substantial terms and representing the world's principal legal systems and languages. The judges would not be permitted to take part in any case in which their own state was a party. There was no substantial opposition to this proposal. The main stumbling block was the inability of the conference to devise an equitable method of selecting the judges.[15]

In the end, the conference drafted 14 conventions. Twelve of these dealt with the conduct of war, and one made minor adjustments in the Convention for the Pacific Settlement of International Disputes. One convention, to create an International Prize Court to deal with merchant ships and cargoes seized in the conduct of hostilities, could have resulted in the world's first international court, but the convention was not ratified by a single state. Although the conference was unable to come to an agreement on compulsory adjudication or the establishment of a true international court, it did make substantial progress in its discussions, and many expected that a third Hague conference would yield agreements on these matters. However, World War I intervened and a third conference was never held. Further work on the creation of a world court would have to await the Paris Peace Conference that ended World War I.

4. Central American Court of Justice

On December 20, 1907, only two months after the conclusion of the second Hague conference five nations, Costa Rica, El Salvador, Guatemala, Honduras, and Nicaragua signed a convention for establishment of the Central American Court of Justice. The convention was rapidly ratified and on May 15, 1908, the world's first international court came into existence. The court was composed of one judge appointed by each of the five states. The court had jurisdiction over all controversies which might arise among the contracting states. In addition, a conflict between one of the five nations and any other nation could be submitted to the court by special agreement between the nations affected. Individuals were permitted to be parties before the court—a national of one country could sue another state for violations of treaties or international law irrespective of whether the individual's own state supported the claim.

The Central American Court successfully resolved a number of controversies. However, the court was established for a term of only ten years, and it was not renewed. There are several reasons why the Central American nations did not continue the court. The provision

15/ The larger nations felt that they should have greater representation on the court than the smaller nations. The smaller nations, on the other hand, were unwilling to agree to a court in which they would feel under represented. One proposal was to have the major powers each appoint one judge with the smaller nations being placed into one of several groups with each group appointing a single judge. A variation on this would have had the major nations appointing a judge for a full 12 year term while the twelve year term of other judges would be divided up among a group of smaller nations. Each would appoint one judge to serve part of the term, *i.e.*, twelve small nations might each appoint a judge for one year of the term and several medium sized nations might appoint a judge for several years of the term. Another proposal had the Permanent Court of Arbitration electing the court from among its members. The U.S. proposed that each nation nominate one candidate for judge. Each nation would then vote by submitting a list of fifteen of the nominees to a central bureau. The fifteen candidates having the greatest number of votes would be elected. This proposal was defeated by a 2/3 majority. *Id.* ¶¶ 65—73.

allowing individuals to initiate cases led to a number of meritless cases that appear to have been politically motivated. In addition, many disputes between the Central American states also involved third nations. For example, one case involved the legality of a treaty between Nicaragua and the U.S. The difficulty of administering justice when a court does not have jurisdiction over all interested states is a problem that continues to plague the ICJ today. In addition, over a short period of time some states are bound to lose more cases than they win. When that happens, they may conclude that they would have been better off without the court. If the court had been continued for a longer period of time such nations might have recognized that the advantages of order and justice outweigh occasional losses before the court. Another reason that the court was not continued may have been that a true worldwide international court was on the horizon.[16]

5. The Permanent Court of International Justice

The five great powers, the United States, Japan, Italy, France, and the United Kingdom, convened the Paris Peace Conference on January 18, 1919. Besides drafting the terms that would end the World War, the conference designed new international institutions that it hoped would prevent future wars. In addition to establishing the League of Nations, the Treaty of Versailles provided in Article 14 that:

> The Council shall formulate and submit to the members of the League for adoption plans for the establishment of a Permanent Court of International Justice. The Court shall be competent to hear and determine any dispute of an international character which the parties thereto submit to it. The Court may also give an advisory opinion upon any dispute or question referred to it by the Council or by the Assembly.[17]

On February 13, 1920, the League appointed an Advisory Committee of Jurists to draw up plans for the Permanent Court that included Elihu Root, former U.S. Secretary of State. The scope of the new court's jurisdiction was a major point of controversy. After much debate, the draft statute prepared by the committee would grant the Court jurisdiction over cases of a legal nature involving (a) the interpretation of treaties, (b) questions of international law, (c) whether a fact exists which would constitute a violation of international law (d) the nature or extent of reparation to be made for breach of an international obligation, and (e) the interpretation of any court judgment. The draft also provided for a measure of compulsory jurisdiction—namely that if a dispute could not be settled by diplomatic means and if the parties did not agree to another method of settlement, the party complaining could submit the case to the Court.

16/ *Id.* ¶¶ 75—79. In 1923 these five Central American nations drafted a convention to reestablish the Central American Court, in a modified form, but the convention never came into force. In that same year, the fifth Pan-American Conference also considered establishing a court for the Western Hemisphere. *Id.* ¶¶ 291—95.

17/ Article 12 of the Treaty of Versailles provided that members of the League should refer any dispute likely to lead to a "rupture" to arbitration, judicial settlement, or enquiry by the Council. Article 13 provided that any dispute which cannot be settled by diplomatic means should be submitted to arbitration or judicial settlement if it is suitable for settlement by such means. The parties further agreed to carry out any settlement that might be ordered.

This proposal proved too advanced for the international community. The League rejected the committee's proposal for compulsory jurisdiction.[18] Instead, the Statute as adopted, provided that the Court could hear cases where a separate treaty provided that the court would have jurisdiction or where a dispute was specifically referred to the Court by the parties. The Statute also contained an "optional clause" that permitted states to file declarations agreeing to accept the jurisdiction of the Court under specified conditions with respect to other states that have filed similar declarations.[19]

On December 16, 1920, the protocol to the Statute was opened for signature. Forty-six nations promptly signed it and by the next meeting of the Assembly, 28 nations had ratified the Statute and it came into force. The first judges were elected in September 1921 and the Court held its first meeting in January 1922. Although an American always served as a judge on the PCIJ, the U.S. never ratified the protocol.

6. The International Court of Justice

Despite its jurisdictional limitations, the PCIJ enjoyed considerable success. In its brief life, it decided 38 contentious cases and issued 28 advisory opinions. Nonetheless, like the League, the PCIJ did not survive the turmoil of World War II. The concept of international adjudication, however, did survive. It played an important part in the negotiations that led to establishment of the United Nations, and the PCIJ was reincarnated as the International Court of Justice. Unlike the PCIJ which was established by separate protocol and was somewhat loosely tied to the League, the ICJ was made the principal judicial organ of the U.N., with all members of the U.N. being parties to the ICJ Statute.[20] Except for this structural difference, in most respects the new Court is a continuation of the PCIJ.[21] For example, the Statute provides that treaties providing for adjudication by the PCIJ shall apply to the ICJ and that acceptances of jurisdiction under the optional clause of the PCIJ shall also apply to the optional clause of the ICJ.[22] The ICJ also took over the Permanent Court's quarters at the Peace Palace in The Hague.

The same procedures are required to amend the ICJ Statute as to amend the U.N. Charter. A vote of two-thirds of the General Assembly and ratification by two-thirds of the members, including all five permanent members of the Security Council, is required. This

---

18/ The advisory committee also recommended establishment of a High Court of International Justice that would be competent to try individuals accused of international crimes. The League was also unwilling to accept this proposal. For a discussion of proposals to create an international criminal court see B. MacPherson, An International Criminal Court—Applying World Law to Individuals (1992) (Monograph #10 published by the Center for U.N. Reform Education).

19/ PCIJ Statute, Art. 36. *See* Part V(C), *infra.*

20/ Article 93 of the Charter provides that nations that are not members of the U.N. may also become parties to the ICJ's Statute.

21/ In preparing for the San Francisco Conference, the Committee of Jurists developed two proposals for compulsory jurisdiction. One retained the optional clause and the other would have given the Court compulsory jurisdiction over all legal disputes. The majority of states represented at the Conference favored full compulsory jurisdiction, but the opposition by the U.S., the Soviet Union, and the United Kingdom forced retention of the optional clause.

22/ Statute, Arts. 36(5) & 37.

procedure is cumbersome, and it would probably be difficult at this time to obtain sufficient support for substantial changes in the Court's Statute.

C. The United States and the Court

1. Traditional U.S. Support of Arbitration

Americans were part of the movement to encourage arbitration and to establish a standing international court.[23] The U.S. embraced arbitration nearly from its inception. In 1794 Secretary of State John Jay negotiated a treaty with Great Britain that established three arbitration panels to resolve a variety of pending disputes.[24] In 1844, the Massachusetts legislature adopted a resolution encouraging the federal government to work toward the establishment of an international tribunal, and the Vermont legislature took similar action in 1852.[25] Then in 1871, a treaty with Great Britain established four arbitration panels to resolve property disputes arising from the Civil War. The most important of these arbitrations involved claims by the U.S. for damages resulting from Britain's role in the activities of the *Alabama,* a British-built ship used by Confederate forces to raid Union ships and cargoes. The *Alabama* arbitration involved an important procedural innovation—the use of neutral judges—three of the five judges were appointed by the President of the Swiss Confederation, the King of Italy, and the Emperor of Brazil. The panel found that Britain violated the rules of neutrality and awarded the U.S. $15.5 million in damages. The U.S. engaged in a number of other successful arbitrations around the turn of the century.

These arbitrations were all conducted pursuant to special agreements that specified the subject matter and rules of the arbitration. In 1897, encouraged by the success of arbitrations between the U.S. and the U.K., Secretary of State Richard Olney and British Ambassador Julian Pauncefote negotiated a five year general arbitration treaty. The Olney-Pauncefote treaty committed the parties to arbitrate all disputes that could not be resolved through diplomatic means, and it specified the procedure for selecting the arbitrators. This was a bold step. Rather than piecemeal submission to arbitration of existing disputes where all the issues are known in advance, this treaty would provide for arbitration of future unknown disputes. It was a step that the Senate was unwilling to take. The Senate criticized the treaty's failure to exempt from mandatory arbitration matters of national honor, territorial integrity, and domestic policy. In addition, under the Constitution, the Senate must, as with all other treaties and international agreements, ratify special arbitration agreements by a two-thirds majority. However, upon ratification of a general arbitration treaty, further Senate approval would not be

---

23/ T. Franck & J. Lehrman, *Messianism & Chauvinism in America's Commitment to Peace Through Law* IN THE INTERNATIONAL COURT OF JUSTICE AT A CROSSROADS 3, 8—12 (L. Damrosch ed. 1987) [hereinafter CROSSROADS].

24/ Treaty of Amity, Commerce & Navigation, Nov. 11, 1794, United States-Great Britain, 8 Stat. 116, T.S. 105. The arbitrations successfully resolved a number of issues that could have lead to a resumption of hostilities. These issues included the location of the St. Croix River boundary and monetary claims related to the Revolutionary War and the British-French War.

25/ BUSTAMANTE, *supra* note 6, at ¶¶ 26 & 41.

required to submit specific disputes to arbitration. The Senate objected to this loss of control, and rejected the treaty.[26]

John Hay, Secretary of State under President McKinley and later under Theodore Roosevelt, presented a detailed plan to the first Hague Conference for a true international court. The U.S. submitted a similarly ambitious proposal to the second Hague Conference. As noted above, neither Conference was ready to create a true international court. Instead the first Hague Conference drafted an agreement to create the Permanent Court of Arbitration. The U.S. Senate found nothing objectionable in this agreement and it was rapidly ratified. President Theodore Roosevelt wanted the U.S. to be the first nation to utilize the procedures under the Hague agreement, and Secretary Hay obtained the agreement of Mexico to submit a case to arbitration.[27]

The State Department, under the direction of Secretary Hay, negotiated eleven bilateral general arbitration treaties in 1903 and 1904 that would oblige the parties to arbitrate future disputes, other than those involving vital interests, independence, or national honor.[28] The Senate, still not enamored with the idea of compulsory arbitration, refused to ratify the treaties unless they included provisions requiring Senate approval before any particular case could be arbitrated—a requirement that is the antithesis of general arbitration treaties. The purpose of general arbitration treaties is to agree in advance to arbitration of specified classes of disputes. To condition such arbitrations upon the consent of either party would accomplish nothing since even in the absence of a general treaty the parties could agree to an arbitration of a particular dispute. Since the condition required by the Senate would defeat the purpose of the treaties, President Roosevelt withdrew them. Several years later, however, Elihu Root, the new Secretary of State, convinced Roosevelt to accept 25 treaties that required Senate consent for any arbitration. His thinking may have been that even though these treaties had little substance, they were better than no arbitration treaties at all.

2. Isolationism Prevents the U.S. from Joining the PCIJ

There was substantially greater sentiment in the U.S. for joining the PCIJ than there was for joining the League of Nations. Many influential Americans who opposed the League favored joining the Court. Nonetheless, the same isolationist sentiments that kept the U.S. out of the League ultimately prevented the Senate from ratifying the Court's Statute. In 1923, despite the urging of President Harding and Secretary of State Charles Evans Hughes, the Senate declined by a two-to-one majority to even consider the question. The Senate did not

---

26/ The U.S. Senate was not alone in being reluctant to ratify general arbitration treaties. In 1890, the First Pan-American Conference drafted an arbitration convention for the hemisphere that was praised by President Benjamin Harrison. However, not a single country ratified the agreement. Treaty of Arbitration, April 28, 1990, in 3 UNPERFECTED TREATIES OF THE U.S. 209 (C. Wiktor ed. 1977).

27/ Pious Fund Arbitration (U.S. - Mexico), 1902 For. Rel. U.S. 15 (Appendix 2) (1903). The arbitration resulted in an award in favor of the U.S.

28/ The Treaties were with France, Switzerland, Germany, Portugal, Great Britain, Italy, Spain, Austria-Hungary, Mexico, Sweden and Norway, and Japan. 3 UNPERFECTED TREATIES OF THE U.S. at 475—499; 4 UNPERFECTED TREATIES OF THE U.S. at 1—23. "National honor" is so vague that the exclusion of matters of national honor from these treaties might, in itself, have made them relatively useless.

In 1911, the U.S. negotiated broad arbitration treaties with France and Great Britain. Again the Senate so eviscerated these treaties that President Taft did not even seek a vote on them.

take up consideration of the PCIJ until December 1925. After substantial debate, the Senate finally ratified the PCIJ protocol on January 27, 1926. However, that ratification contained a reservation introduced by Senator Borah, an opponent of the Court, that the PCIJ should not, without the consent of the U.S., entertain any request by the League for an advisory opinion on any matter in which the U.S. had an interest. This condition, which would give the U.S. alone a veto power over requests for advisory opinions, was unacceptable to the League. In order to give the U.S. parity with other League members, a compromise was proposed that would give an objection by the U.S. to a request for an advisory opinion the same effect as a negative vote by a member of the League. The Senate rejected this compromise in 1935. While 52 Senators voted in favor of joining the Court, and 36 against, this was still seven votes shy of the necessary two-thirds majority required for ratification.

> [W]e favor, and have always favored, an international court of justice for the determination according to judicial standards of judicable international disputes.
>
> *Secretary of State*
> *Charles Evans Hughes*
> *(October 30, 1922)*

3. U.S. Leadership Leads to Creation of the U.N. and the ICJ

In discussions leading to the U.N. Charter, most nations favored compulsory jurisdiction for the new ICJ. However, the U.S. joined with the Soviet Union to block making ICJ jurisdiction compulsory. They preferred retention of the optional clause. Nonetheless, the U.S. delegates indicated that once the U.S. joined the U.N., the administration would work toward acceptance of jurisdiction under the optional clause. U.S. officials may have feared that presenting both U.N. membership and compulsory ICJ jurisdiction as a single item would be too much for the Senate to swallow. Senator Wayne Morse of Oregon led the fight for U.S. acceptance of jurisdiction under the optional clause. On the day that the Senate ratified the U.N. Charter, he introduced a resolution urging the President to accept the optional clause. The Senate did not consider this resolution and he introduced another in November. This second resolution contained two additional provisions. First, it specified that the declaration could be terminated upon six months notice. Second, it contained reservations that excluded matters that were entrusted by agreement to resolution by other tribunals and matters which are essentially within the domestic jurisdiction of the U.S.

All witnesses at the hearings testified in favor of compulsory jurisdiction. Nonetheless, a number of Senators remained wary of an unrestrained grant of compulsory jurisdiction to the ICJ. Senator Vandenberg offered an amendment limiting jurisdiction in cases involving disputes based upon multilateral treaties. Senator Connally of Texas introduced an amendment to the draft domestic jurisdiction reservation specifying that the reservation excludes domestic matters "as determined by the United States of America." By making the U.S. the sole judge of whether a dispute is within the domestic jurisdiction of the U.S., this reservation rendered the declaration nearly meaningless. Nevertheless, these amendments were accepted, and on August 2, 1946, the Senate passed a resolution accepting the ICJ's compulsory jurisdiction by a vote of 60 to 2, and it was submitted to the Secretary-General on August 26.

> While it would be foolish to suppose that litigation before the Court is the answer to all the world's problems, this could profitably be employed in a wider range of cases than is presently done. . . . Clearly all disputes regarding domestic matters must remain permanently within the jurisdiction of our own courts. . . . But the United States reserved the right to determine unilaterally whether the subject matter of a particular dispute is within the domestic jurisdiction of the United States and is therefore excluded from the jurisdiction of the Court. As a result of this position, . . . other nations have adopted similar reservations. This is one of the major reasons for the lack of judicial business before the Court. To remedy this situation, the Administration will shortly submit to the Congress recommendations for modifying this reservation. It is our hope that by taking the initiative in this way, other countries may be persuaded to accept and agree to a wider jurisdiction of the International Court.
>
> *Vice President Richard Nixon*
> *Address to the Academy of Political Science*
> *(April 13, 1959)*

Under the Constitution the executive branch is primarily responsible for U.S. foreign policy. The Senate, however, plays an essential role since it must ratify treaties and similar international agreements by a two-thirds majority. U.S. Presidents and Secretaries of State, from the Harrison to Carter administrations, have been among the strongest proponents of third-party adjudication of international disputes, either by arbitration or by an international court. Presidents Eisenhower, Kennedy, Johnson, Nixon, and Ford all favored repeal of the Connally reservation. Their progressive efforts have often been frustrated by the Senate, which has remained reluctant to commit the U.S. to compulsory adjudication. Nonetheless, on May 9, 1974, the Senate passed a resolution calling upon the Secretary of State to study ways of widening access to the ICJ to include individuals, corporations, non-governmental organizations, and regional organizations. The State Department issued its report in October 1976.[29] The Report stated that "the single most significant step by the United States toward promoting a more supportive approach to the Court would be its repeal of the Connally Amendment."[30] Other recommendations included allowing the U.N. to be a party to cases before the ICJ and permitting national courts and additional international organizations to request advisory opinions. The report was skeptical about the willingness of the world community to permit individuals to appear as parties before the Court.

The U.S. has been a party to a number of contentious cases. These cases are summarized in the table on pages 16—17. As indicated in the table, a number of applications filed by the U.S. have been dismissed for lack of jurisdiction. Of those cases for which the ICJ found jurisdiction, the U.S. has won about as many as it has lost. In addition, the U.S. has

---

29/ Department of State, Widening Access to the International Court of Justice (1976), *reprinted in part in*, 16 I.L.M. 187 [hereinafter 1976 State Department Report].

30/ 16 I.L.M. at 189.

had an interest in a number of advisory opinions.[31] In nearly all of the advisory proceedings, the Court's determinations have been in substantial agreement with the U.S. position.[32]

4. U.S. Retrenchment Arising from the *Nicaragua* Case

The Reagan administration was the first in recent years to be actively hostile to the ICJ's compulsory jurisdiction.[33] This hostility was prompted by Nicaragua commencing a case against the U.S. on April 9, 1984. Nicaragua alleged that the U.S. had violated customary international law and its obligations under a Friendship, Commerce, and Navigation (FCN) treaty by mining Nicaraguan waters and by supporting Contra forces that were fighting the Nicaraguan government. The U.S. justified its actions against Nicaragua on the ground that they were a reasonable exercise of the right of collective self defense to defend El Salvador and other Central American nations from Nicaraguan aggression. The U.S., having learned of Nicaragua's intentions in advance, attempted on April 6 to modify its acceptance of jurisdiction under the optional clause to exclude disputes involving Central America.

The Court granted Nicaragua's request for preliminary measures on May 10, 1984. These measures directed the U.S. to cease mining or otherwise blocking access to Nicaraguan ports and to respect Nicaragua's sovereignty.[34] On October 4, 1984, the Court denied El Salvador's petition to intervene in the jurisdiction and admissibility phase of the proceeding, but indicated that El Salvador could pursue intervention in the merits phase.

The Court delivered its decision on jurisdiction and admissibility on November 26, 1984. The Court found that the U.S. attempt to modify its declaration under the optional clause to exclude Central American disputes did not deprive it of jurisdiction because the U.S. declaration by its terms could be terminated only upon six months notice. The Court also rejected the U.S. contentions that Nicaragua had not validly accepted the ICJ's jurisdiction under the optional clause and that the FCN treaty did not apply to the present dispute. Finally, the Court found no merit to the U.S. position that the case was inadmissible on the ground that the Security Council has exclusive jurisdiction over disputes involving the use of force. Accordingly, the Court found that it had jurisdiction and that the case was admissible.

On January 18, 1985, the Reagan administration issued a statement in which it strongly disagreed with the Court's decisions on jurisdiction and El Salvador's petition to intervene.[35]

31/ For example, the U.S. was primarily responsible for seeking the advisory opinion in *Interpretation of Peace Treaties with Bulgaria, Hungary & Romania*, 1950 I.C.J. 221. Bulgaria, Hungary and Romania had violated human rights violations in their peace treaties with the U.S., and they refused to cooperate in the dispute settlement provisions in the treaties. The Court advised that while the parties did have an obligation to cooperate in the dispute settlement provisions, the U.S. could not substitute new settlement provisions for those in the treaties. The affected states did not comply with the opinion.

32/ G. Butcher, *The Consonance of U.S. Positions with the International Court's Advisory Opinions*, in CROSSROADS, *supra* note 23, at 423, 443-46.

33/ Ironically, Republican presidents have been the strongest supporters of the Court, while some Democratic presidents, such as Wilson and Franklin Roosevelt, have been less enthusiastic about the value of a world court.

34/ 1984 I.C.J. 169.

35/ Statement Concerning U.S. Withdrawal from the *Nicaragua* Case (Jan. 18, 1985), *reprinted in* 24 I.L.M. 246 *and* CROSSROADS, *supra* note 23, at Annex E.

CONTENTIOUS CASES INVOLVING THE UNITED STATES

Rights of Nationals in Morocco (France v. U.S.), 1952 I.C.J 176 (Merits). (Jurisdiction — Optional Clause).

The case concerned rights granted to U.S. nationals under several treaties from the 18th and 19th centuries. In 1917 France obtained a mandate over Morocco and asked other nations to give up all special rights that Morocco had previously granted. The U.S. declined and protested when in 1946 Morocco adopted trade legislation favoring France over the U.S. The U.S. welcomed France's suit as a means of resolving this long standing dispute. Most issues were resolved in favor of the U.S.

Monetary Gold Removed from Rome in 1943 (Italy v. France, U.K. & U.S.), 1954 I.C.J. 19 (Merits) [Hereinafter *Monetary Gold*]. (Jurisdiction — Special Agreement).

Albanian gold seized by Germany during World War II was in the hands of a commission composed of the U.S., the U.K. and France. The commission agreed among themselves that the gold would be given to the U.K. in partial satisfaction of the unsatisfied judgment in the *Corfu Channel* case unless Italy or Albania instituted proceedings before the ICJ. Italy initiated this case and asserted that the Court could not exercise jurisdiction in the absence of Albania. The ICJ agreed, finding in the preliminary objection stage that Albania was an indispensable party. The U.S. did not have any significant interest in the outcome of the case.

Interhandle (Switzerland v. U.S.), 1957 I.C.J. 105 (Preliminary Objections), 1959 I.C.J. 6 (Merits). (Jurisdiction — Optional Clause).

The U.S. seized the assets of Interhandle under the Trading With the Enemy Act. Switzerland protested that the company was Swiss and neutral. At the preliminary objection phase, the case was held inadmissible because domestic remedies had not been exhausted.

Aerial Incident of 27 July 1955 (U.S. v. Bulgaria), 1960 I.C.J. 146 (Dismissal Order) (Jurisdiction — Optional Clause).

An Israeli civil aircraft that included U.S. citizens among its passengers was shot down when it penetrated Bulgarian airspace. The U.S. withdrew the case after Bulgaria invoked its reciprocal rights under the Connally Amendment to the U.S. declaration.

U.S. Diplomatic & Consular Staff in Tehran (U.S. v. Iran), 1979 I.C.J. 7 (Provisional Measures), 1980 I.C.J. 3 (Merits) [hereinafter *Hostages*]. (Jurisdiction — Compromissory Clause).

The U.S. embassy together with U.S. diplomats and other nationals were seized by Iran. Iran refused to appear in the case and did not comply with the order for provisional measures. The Court found for the U.S., holding that Iran's actions violated several treaties and customary international law. It ordered release of the hostages and reparations to be paid to the U.S. If the parties did not reach an agreement on reparations, they would be determined by the Court. The dispute was subsequently settled.

Delimitation of the Maritime Boundary in the Gulf of Maine Area (Canada/U.S.), 1982 I.C.J. 3 (Constitution of Chamber), 1984 I.C.J. 246 (Merits) [hereinafter *Gulf of Maine*]. (Jurisdiction — Special Agreement).

Pursuant to an agreement, a special chamber of the Court resolved a longstanding boundary dispute in the Gulf of Maine, with neither side receiving everything it asked for.

Military & Paramilitary Activities in & Against Nicaragua (Nicaragua v. U.S.), 1984 I.C.J. 169 (Provisional Measures), 1984 I.C.J. 215 (Intervention), 1984 I.C.J. 392 (Jurisdiction & Admissibility), 1986 I.C.J. 14 (Merits) [hereinafter *Nicaragua*]. (Jurisdiction — Optional & Compromissory Clauses).

Nicaragua initiated the proceeding alleging that the U.S. violated customary international law and its treaty obligations by mining its harbors and by supporting contra forces seeking overthrow of its government. After adverse ruling on jurisdiction and admissibility, the U.S. withdrew its participation in the case. On the merits, the Court found for Nicaragua on most issues. After a change in government, Nicaragua withdrew the case.

Elettronica Sicula S.p.A (ELSI) (U.S.-Italy), 1988 I.C.J. 158 (Constitution of Chamber), 1989 I.C.J. 15 (Merits) [hereinafter *ELSI*]. (Jurisdiction — Compromissory Clause).

Proceeding involved a dispute involving an Italian firm owned by a U.S. corporation. Italian bankruptcy and other actions caused the loss of the firm. A chamber of the Court ruled in favor of Italy.

Aerial Incident of 3 July 1988 (Iran v. U.S.), (Jurisdiction — Compromissory Clause) (Case is Pending).

An Iranian aircraft with 290 people on board was shot down over the Persian Gulf by the USS Vincennes. Iran seeks reparations for loss of the aircraft and the individuals on board.

Questions of Interpretation & Application of the 1971 Montreal Convention Arising from the Aerial Incident at Lockerbie (Libya v. U.S. & U.K.), 1992 I.C.J. 114 (Provisional Measures) [hereinafter *Lockerbie*]. (Jurisdiction — Compromissory Clause) (Case is Pending).

The U.S. and the U.K. indicted two Libyans for downing Pan Am Flight 103 above Lockerbie, Scotland, and demanded their extradition from Libya. Libya contends that under the Montreal Convention, it has the right to try the accused in its own courts. Libya seeks to prevent the U.S. and U.K. from pressuring it to extradite the accused, including blocking the U.S. and U.K. from seeking sanctions from the Security Council. The ICJ denied Libya's request for provisional measures.

Case Concerning Oil Platforms (Iran v. U.S.) (Jurisdiction — Compromissory Clause) (Case is Pending).

The case concerns the destruction by the U.S. of Iranian oil platforms in the Persian Gulf.

The U.S. filed the following applications where no arguable basis for jurisdiction existed either for political purposes or in the hope that the defendant states would accept having the case heard by the ICJ:

Treatment in Hungary of Aircraft & Crew of USA (U.S. v. Hung. & USSR), 1954 I.C.J. 99 & 103.

Aerial Incident of March 10, 1953 (U.S. v. Czechoslovakia), 1956 I.C.J. 6.

Aerial Incident of October 7, 1952 (U.S. v. USSR), 1956 I.C.J. 9.

Aerial Incident of September 4, 1954 (U.S. v. U.S.S.R), 1958 I.C.J. 158.

Aerial Incident of November 7, 1954 (U.S. v. U.S.S.R.), 1959 I.C.J. 276.

It announced that the U.S. would not participate further in the proceeding. This was followed, on October 7, 1985, by withdrawal of the U.S. declaration accepting compulsory jurisdiction under the optional clause.[36] In the statement accompanying the October 7 notice, the State Department explained that U.S. experience with compulsory jurisdiction had been unsatisfactory, in that the U.S. had never been able to bring a case under the optional clause but had itself been sued three times. The State Department reiterated its belief that the ICJ's acceptance of the *Nicaragua* case was improper and that the Court's process was being abused for political ends. The statement explained that in view of uncertainties over whether the Court would properly apply the optional clause, continued acceptance of "compulsory jurisdiction would be contrary to our commitment to the principle of equal application of the law and would endanger our vital national interests." The statement emphasized that its complaint was with the way that the Court deals with compulsory jurisdiction and that the U.S. retains its commitment to the ICJ when it is performing its "proper functions." It stated that the U.S. will "continue to make use of the Court whenever appropriate," including cases where treaties provide for ICJ resolution of disputes. To emphasize this point, on the same day that the U.S. withdrew its declaration under the optional clause, it announced an agreement with Italy to submit the *ELSI* case to the Court.

In view of the withdrawal of the U.S. from the *Nicaragua* proceeding, that case proceeded without the benefit of U.S. participation. On June 27, 1986, the ICJ reached a decision on the merits that found for Nicaragua on most issues.[37] The Court deferred consideration of the amount of reparations to be paid to Nicaragua to a subsequent stage of the proceeding. However, before a decision was reached on reparations, the government of Nicaragua changed to one more favorable to the U.S., and on September 12, 1991, the case was dismissed at Nicaragua's request.

The Central American conflict out of which the *Nicaragua* case arose was controversial within the U.S., and a person's view of that conflict is likely to color their opinion of the *Nicaragua* proceeding. The conflict has largely been resolved. In addition, the report of the U.N. Truth Commission which found the El Salvador government to have engaged in extensive human rights violations has led many who previously supported the U.S. policy of assisting El Salvador to now question that policy. As a result, the *Nicaragua* case can be expected to engender less emotion and play a smaller role in the formulation of future U.S. policy toward the Court.

Moreover, U.S. hostility toward compulsory jurisdiction was largely the product of the Reagan and Bush administrations. U.S. foreign policy can change radically with a change in administrations. How President Clinton and Secretary of State Christopher will deal with the Court remains an open question. In September 1993 the U.S. Commission on Improving the Effectiveness of the United Nations issued its report. That report called for increased utilization of the ICJ, including wider acceptance of compulsory jurisdiction by member states and expansion of the Court's advisory jurisdiction. Hopefully, this report will prompt the administration to take progressive action to increase U.S. use and support of the Court.

36/ Notice of Termination of the 1946 Declaration (Oct. 7, 1985), *reprinted in* CROSSROADS, *supra* note 23, at Annex F.

37/ On July 28, 1986, Nicaragua initiated proceedings against Costa Rica and Honduras, in which it alleged that they also violated international law through involvement in armed actions across their borders.

III. The Role of the Court in Dispute Settlement

A. Utilization of the Court

At the time it was established, the World Court was expected to play a pivotal role in the maintenance of international peace. Some speculated that an effective court would entirely eliminate resort to war. It was assumed that nations would welcome the opportunity to resolve their disputes on the basis of law and would voluntarily comply with adverse judgments. These expectations proved unrealistic. No court alone can abolish war any more than the U.S. Supreme Court could prevent the Civil War. Moreover, the effectiveness of the Court suffers because of its lack of compulsory jurisdiction and because it is not part of a complete legal system that includes a method of legislating law and of enforcing the court's judgments. Only a complete legal system would have any chance of ensuring peace.

Nonetheless, even with its limitations, the World Court has the capacity to play a far greater role in the search for peace than it has played to date. It has been seriously underutilized. Fewer than 160 cases, including requests for advisory opinions, have been referred to the Court since it was established in 1922 under the League of Nations, and many of these were dismissed for lack of jurisdiction or because the underlying dispute was settled before the Court issued its decision. Moreover, most of them involved relatively minor disputes that were unlikely to lead to hostilities. Nations have been especially reluctant to refer major controversies to the Court even when they involve factual and legal issues that are appropriate for adjudication. For example:

- Disagreements arose soon after the 1954 Geneva Accord which ended the fighting in Vietnam in the early 1950's. The treaty called for the eventual unification of Vietnam under free elections to be held in 1956. The North accused the South of refusing to permit the elections and the South accused the North of infiltration and terrorism that would have made elections a mockery. Instead of seeking mediation or enquiry, and if they failed asking the ICJ to resolve this dispute, North and South Vietnam went to war. The war eventually entangled the U.S. and cost over one million lives.
- A dispute over the right of free passage through the Suez Canal and the Gulf of Aquaba in 1967 could have been litigated in the ICJ, but instead war broke out.
- The United Kingdom and Argentina fought a war costing about 1,000 lives over the ownership of the Falkland (Malvinas) islands—an issue that could have been submitted to the Court.
- The Gulf War involved in part a boundary dispute between Iraq and Kuwait and allegations that Kuwait was stealing Iraq's oil through slant drilling across the border. These disputes could have been decided by the ICJ and a war costing over 100,000 lives and horrendous environmental damage might have been prevented.

Whether war could have been averted in any of these cases would have depended upon the willingness of the parties to accept an adverse decision. Nonetheless, peaceful resolution through the ICJ should have been tried instead of resorting to war.

B. When Is Adjudication Appropriate?

Adjudication is only one method of resolving disputes. The important thing is not the number of cases submitted to the Court, but whether international disputes are being resolved fairly and peacefully. The best method of settlement in one situation may not be the best in another. Adjudication, whether before a court or before an arbitral tribunal, has certain advantages and disadvantages over negotiated settlements. States weigh many factors when deciding on the most appropriate way to resolve a particular international dispute.[38]

We live in a relatively small but highly interrelated world. The parties to a dispute will have to continue dealing with each other long after the dispute is settled. The American people are among the most litigious on earth, and we often look first to the courts as a means of settling domestic disputes. In many cultures, however, courts are resorted to only in rare circumstances. Indeed, even in the U.S., many businessmen recognize that a mutually acceptable settlement may be more desirable than litigation. Consequently, before a state seeks to impose adjudication on an unwilling adversary, it should consider its effect on relations between them. A negotiated compromise may be more desirable in some circumstances than a judicial decision vindicating a state's full legal rights. Of course, a mutual agreement to submit a dispute to adjudication should not harm relations and may remove a possible irritant to those relations.

> [C]ourts are designed to apply law, not make it, and international law has not yet developed the scope and definiteness necessary to permit international disputes generally to be resolved by judicial rather than political tests.
>
> *John Foster Dulles*
> *Senate Hearings on Compulsory Jurisdiction (1946)*

States that believe they have winning cases are most likely to desire adjudication. In making this determination, a state's assessment of the applicable law is critical. The Court enforces treaties and applies customary international law. However, customary international law is in a relatively early stage of development, and there are many areas in which there is no clear rule of conduct. Uncertainty about the applicable law, as well as doubts about whether the court will be able to obtain necessary evidence, tend to discourage adjudication. Moreover, customary international law is slow to change and a state

38/ *See generally* R. Bilder, *Some Limitations of Adjudication as an International Dispute Resolution Technique,* 23 VA J. INT'L L. 1 (1982); R. Bilder, *International Dispute Settlement & the Role of International Adjudication,* in CROSSROADS, *supra* note 23, at 155.

may sincerely believe that a current rule of customary law is unjust and wrong.[39] For example, one of the reasons that the U.S. withdrew from the *Nicaragua* case may have been that it believed that the rule concerning assistance to irregular or revolutionary forces is outdated.[40] The fact that the ICJ is not part of a complete legal system that includes a method of legislating or updating international law may hinder use of the Court, since it may lead the Court to apply outdated rules. Establishment of an effective method of lawmaking might lead to greater acceptance by the world community of international law and to increased willingness of states to utilize the ICJ.

> [No one] would for a moment have expected any domestic court within a State to be able of itself to create order in society by the rule of law when isolated from other organs of government . . . . For even in a developed society working within the legal system of a state, it may be found wiser and even compelling on occasion, to change anachronistic or outdated law rather than seek to enforce it through the courts. There are, therefore, some situations . . . which require a political decision . . . rather than a decision by a court on the basis of existing law. It is a source of constant wonder that so many good people . . . could suppose that an international court with compulsory jurisdiction was really possible without complimentary . . . competencies vested in other kinds of governmental bodies.
>
> *ICJ President Sir Robert Jennings*
> *Address to the General Assembly (1991)*

Any litigation, whether in the World Court or in domestic courts, involves risk of an adverse decision. With negotiated settlements the parties maintain control, since neither party has to accept a settlement that it finds unacceptable. Whether a party is willing to surrender this control and risk a politically undesirable decision by accepting adjudication may depend upon the nature of the dispute and the depth of its desire to avoid further conflict. States tend to be less willing to refer serious matters involving what they believe to be their vital interests to adjudication. But they may do so if the alternative is equally serious. For example, before the Gulf War threatened, Kuwait would probably have been unwilling to accept adjudication on Iraq's claim to all of Kuwait's territory. On the other hand, if the alternative to adjudication appeared to be almost certain occupation by Iraq, adjudication would be much more attractive.

Initiating judicial proceedings may prod stalled settlement negotiations. It may demonstrate that the nation seeking adjudication believes in the justness of its position, and

---

39/ Of course, far too frequently, national leaders do not care whether they act legally. Hitler cared little for legal niceties, although he often accompanied Germany's aggression in World War II with purported "legal' justifications. Similarly, while Saddam Hussein asserted legal "justifications" for Iraq's invasion of Kuwait, it is quite possible that he would have ordered the invasion even if the ICJ had determined that these alleged "justifications" were frivolous. The ICJ can do little about such leaders since they are unlikely to agree to adjudication, and if it is imposed on them, they are unlikely to comply with any adverse judgment.

40/ Under customary international law, nations are permitted to provide military and other assistance to governments, but not to rebels seeking to overthrow established governments, at least until the rebels obtain power or authority comparable to that of the established government. U.S. ambassador to the U.N. Jeane Kirkpatrick urged a change that would allow assistance to democratic forces that were fighting totalitarian forces. This would be the converse to the Soviet policy which contended that assistance to national liberation movements or to Marxist forces was permissible. Franck & Lehrman, *supra* note 23, at 4.

the opposing party may take the matter more seriously resulting in a more flexible negotiating position. Where a dispute is escalating tensions, commencing a Court proceeding may provide a cooling off period that buys time for further negotiations. In other circumstances, however, it might polarize the issues and freeze the parties' positions, making a negotiated settlement impossible. There is also the risk that a Court proceeding will be used for propaganda or harassment.

Many international disputes are not intrinsically important to the parties, but a settlement of them may have serious domestic political repercussions. It may be politically difficult for a government to compromise a dispute that the populace is passionate about or where it could seriously impact a portion of the population. By passing the buck to the ICJ, a government can remove the dispute without appearing responsible for compromising the national interest. The government can avoid blame by taking the position that it is only following international law. For example, the *Gulf of Maine* case involved a dispute between the U.S. and Canada over a maritime boundary. The boundary issue involved the rights to rich fishing grounds, and any negotiated settlement might have been considered a sell-out by both nations' fishing industries. This political hot-potato was successfully passed to the World Court.

Whether adjudication will dispose of the dispute must also be considered. Where negotiation has been unable to resolve a matter, the parties may welcome adjudication as a means of ending the dispute. Oftentimes, however, the direct legal dispute is merely a symptom of a deeper problem. In such cases, if adjudication is unable to deal with the underlying dispute, it would not settle the real controversy. Moreover, if a party chooses to ignore a Court judgment there may be little recourse for the wining state. While it could seek enforcement measures from the Security Council, any one of the permanent members could veto such measures. Consequently, if a losing party refuses to comply voluntarily, an ICJ judgment will often not end the dispute. But even without direct enforcement, an authoritative World Court decision could further settlement by turning world opinion to the support of the aggrieved state. Nevertheless, a negotiated settlement that the other party accepts will frequently be superior to a more favorable Court judgment that becomes a hollow victory.

The decision on whether to seek a judicial determination will also depend upon whether the state has confidence in the Court's impartiality and ability to handle the issues involved in the dispute. If the parties distrust the Court, they may opt for arbitration where they may be able to choose the decision-makers. On the other hand, a court with full time judges might be viewed by some as more independent and professional than part time arbitrators.

Litigation can be expensive and its cost may be a crucial factor, especially for smaller states, in determining whether to seek an adjudicated resolution. The World Court can be cheaper than arbitration since the parties must pay only their own expenses, not the expenses of the Court, while they would have to pay the expenses of an arbitration panel.[41] States that are unfamiliar with the Court's procedures may, on the other hand, feel more comfortable with arbitration where there is greater opportunity to negotiate procedural matters.

Domestic courts may advance the rule of law even when they are not being used. Where compulsory jurisdiction exists, both parties know that the other can always bring suit to have

---

41/ In 1989 the U.N. established the Secretary General's Trust Fund to Assist States in the Settlement of Disputes Through the International Court of Justice. The fund provides financial assistance to poorer states for expenses related to litigation of cases submitted to the Court by special agreements. *See* 28 I.L.M. 1589 (1989); P. Bekker, *International Legal Aid in Practice: The ICJ Trust Fund*, 87 AM. J. INT'L L. 659 (1993).

the case resolved on the basis of the law. The threat of litigation may induce fair settlements based primarily upon the parties' assessments of the legal merits of their positions. In contrast, there is seldom compulsory jurisdiction in the international sphere, and the ICJ cannot level the playing field in the same way as domestic courts. As a result, the relative military, economic and political strengths of the parties may be more important in determining a settlement than are considerations of justice. Strong nations can, like bullies, demand settlements that are more favorable than can be justified by strictly legal considerations. Consequently, major powers tend to favor negotiated settlements. Weaker nations tend to seek refuge in adjudication that will decide their rights according to the law, since in theory at least all nations are equal before the Court. A stronger court system, with universal compulsory jurisdiction and enforceable judgments, could better protect the rights of weaker states and help ensure that disputes are resolved equitably on the basis of law and justice.

IV. THE JUDICIARY

The Court is composed of 15 judges, no two of whom may be citizens of the same state. They are elected for nine year terms and may be reelected. The Statute provides that judges should be elected regardless of their nationality and that in electing them the states should consider that the Court as a whole should represent the main forms of civilization and the principal legal systems of the world.[42]

A. Improving the Selection Process

Nominations are made by the members of the Permanent Court of Arbitration. Each group of members from a given state on the arbitration court are entitled to nominate four persons for the ICJ, not more than two of whom are of their own nationality. States not represented on the Court of Arbitration (a majority of U.N. members) may appoint nominating groups under the same conditions as if they were appointing members to the Court of Arbitration. The statute urges each national nominating group to consult with its "highest court of justice, its legal faculties and schools of law, and its national academies and national sections of international academies." As a practical matter, the U.S. members of the Court of Arbitration generally forward the recommendations of the American Bar Association and the American Society of International Law. Elections are conducted by both the General Assembly and the Security Council (the veto not applying), with a majority vote of both bodies being necessary for election.

The judges are elected at the same time as are members of other U.N. organizations, and consequently, some political bargaining occurs as support for judicial candidates is traded off for support for candidates to other bodies. It is also not unusual for Court candidates to openly lobby for their election. Moreover, while nationality should not be a factor, the Court is in practice selected under the same system of geographical representation that is used in the selection of Security Council members and members of most other bodies in the U.N. system, *i.e.*, one judge from each of the five permanent members of the Security Council; two each from Western Europe, sub-Saharan Africa, Asia and Latin America; and one each from Eastern Europe and the Arabic nations.[43] As a rule, the candidates from each of these regions are

---

42/ The Statute contains a number of provisions designed to limit the chance of bias. Members of the Court are prohibited from exercising any political or administrative function or from engaging in any occupation of a professional nature. Art. 16. Nor may a judge act as a counsel in any case or participate in any proceeding in which he previously had acted as a counsel. Art. 17.

43/ The current make-up of the Court is as follows: Sir Robert Jennings (U.K.) (President), Roberto Ago (Italy), Andres Aguilar Mawdsley (Venez.), Mohammed Bedjaoui (Algeria), Carl-August Fleishhauer (Ger.), Gilbert Guillaume (Fr.), Abdul Koroma (Sierra Leone), Shigeru Oda (Japan), Raymond Ranjeva (Maddagascar), Stephen Schwebel (U.S.), Mohammed Shahabuddeen (Guyana), Jiuyong Shi (China), Nikolai Tarassov (Russia), and Christopher Weeramantry (Sri Lanka).

selected by caucuses of the states from those regions, and the actual elections usually ratify these regional choices.[44]

Although strict geographical distribution of the Court's judges may enhance the political balance of the ICJ, this and the manner in which the elections are in fact conducted contribute to the perception of the Court as a political rather than a judicial body. Early in its history, the ICJ was accused by many countries of having a pro-Western bias, but in recent years the pendulum has swung and it has been accused of having an anti-Western bias. Irrespective of whether these perceptions are correct, they constitute a major impediment to the use of the Court. States will be reluctant to refer disputes to the ICJ if they lack confidence that the Court will render unbiased decisions based upon law rather than political considerations.

On the whole, the Court appears to function as the unbiased tribunal it was intended to be. Certainly, the mere fact that the Court has ruled in a particular way is not in itself evidence of bias. Each judge brings with him a perspective based upon his training and cultural values. A decision based upon a judge's particular conception of the law does not constitute bias, even if that conception is a minority position.[45] Bias exists when a decision is based upon the identity of a party or upon political considerations rather than upon the judge's good faith view of the law.[46] The ICJ's shift in orientation away from the Western perspective appears to result from the greater geographical and philosophical diversity of its membership. In 1946, there were six judges from the Americas, four from Western Europe, and the judges from China and Egypt also had Western European values. Today, only three judges are from the Americas (there are still four from Western Europe). The Court has therefore become more truly international in character in that it reflects the diversity of the world's legal philosophies.

Nonetheless, the method of selecting judges could be improved to reduce the suggestion of bias or politicization. The need of judges to seek reelection has often been pointed to as a weakness in the system. Some commentators maintain that this may tempt judges to follow the position of the electoral group that elected them, especially as the time for reelection draws near. The extent, if any, that reelection pressures influence a judge's votes cannot be determined. This potential problem could be eliminated by giving judges life tenure, as is the case with judges in U.S. federal courts. One alternative is to have a longer term of office

---

44/ F. Morrison, *The Future of International Adjudication,* 75 MINN. L. REV. 827, 841-43 (1991). M. Leigh & S. Ramsey, *Confidence in the Court: It Need Not Be a Hollow Chamber*, in CROSSROADS, *supra* note 23, at 108—09.

45/ The Judges should ensure that they avoid any appearance of bias. The Court generally gives descriptive, yet neutral captions to cases. For example, a case concerning the downing of a civilian airliner by Bulgaria was captioned simply "Aerial Incident of 17 July 1955." Nonetheless, the ICJ refused the U.S.'s request to change the caption of the *Nicaragua* proceeding ("*Military and Paramilitary Activities in and Against Nicaragua*") to a more neutral title. Acceding to this request would have cost the ICJ nothing and would have avoided unnecessarily exacerbating the U.S.'s distrust of the Court. In addition, during the *Nicaragua* proceeding Judge Elias, who was then president of the Court, denounced the U.S. invasion of Grenada as "gunboat diplomacy" and contrary to "behaving according to the rule of law." He noted that "smaller nations wonder what happened to the rule of law when the United States can behave like this." While these comments did not directly relate to the *Nicaragua* case, they formed a basis for questioning Judge Elias's impartiality. Judges should avoid making such injudicious comments.

46/ A recent study of the voting patterns of ICJ judges indicates that they do not vote in any predetermined way and tends to support the proposition that the Court has functioned as intended, *i.e.,* as an independent and impartial judicial body. *See* E. Weiss, *Judicial Independence & Impartiality: A Preliminary Inquiry*, in CROSSROADS, *supra* note 23, at 133.

without the possibility of reelection. But this would not eliminate all potential bias, since a judge might be tempted to rule in favor of his nation's position in order to ensure a position in the government after his term as judge ends.

Removing national governments from the election process could reduce the risk of political influence on the Court. Election of judges by national bar associations or national supreme courts are possibilities, provided the votes of the electors are not dictated by their national governments. Another possibility would be for nations to nominate candidates but have the elections conducted by a body of individuals, perhaps a body such as the International Law Commission, voting by secret ballot independent of their governments.[47] A number of commentators and political figures, especially in the larger nations, have complained that smaller nations have too much say in the composition of the Court. Both the several-fold increase in membership in the U.N. and the increase in the size of the Security Council from 11 to 15 members have diluted the voting strength of the major powers. If elections continue to be conducted by states, some weighted voting system, rather than the current one-nation, one-vote system might be more acceptable to the larger and more powerful states.[48]

Some commentators have recommended that only citizens of states that have accepted the Court's general jurisdiction under the optional clause should be eligible to be judges on the Court.[49] This is founded upon the belief that those states most likely to be litigants should be represented on the Court. It is also intended to encourage states to accept the optional clause.[50] This would be counterproductive. In this writer's view, no individual should be disqualified from being a judge simply because the nation of which he is a national has not accepted compulsory jurisdiction. It would increase the perception of judges as partisan representatives of their nations rather than as independent decision-makers. It would also be difficult to apply in practice given that there is a wide variation in scope of declarations under the optional clause—some of them confer very little jurisdiction on the Court. Moreover, it ignores the fact that while some states may not have accepted the ICJ's general jurisdiction, they may have accepted substantial jurisdiction through compromissory clauses in treaties. If it is thought necessary to encourage states to accept the optional clause, either the right to nominate judicial candidates or the right to vote for judges could be limited to those states accepting the clause, but this might discourage use of the Court through special agreements or compromissory clauses by such states.

47/ A similar proposal was considered for the PCIJ. It would have reversed the present process by having the states nominate the candidates and the Permanent Court of Arbitration elect the judges.

48/ Concerns about voting power are not confined to judicial elections, but include U.N. decisionmaking generally. Some have suggested that the General Assembly be made a democratically elected legislature with proportional representation. Another proposal is the "binding triad." Under this proposal, General Assembly resolutions would become binding law if they are approved by (1) a specified percentage of the number of states, (2) states representing a specified percentage of the world's population, and (3) states representing a specified percentage of the world's economic power. *See generally* R. MORROW, PROPOSALS FOR A MORE EQUITABLE GENERAL ASSEMBLY VOTING STRUCTURE (1989) (Monograph #5 published by the Center for U.N. Reform Education).

49/ L. Gross, *Compulsory Jurisdiction Under the Optional Clause: History & Practice,* in CROSSROADS, *supra* note 23, at 19, 35—42. For a discussion of the optional clause see the next section.

50/ On the other hand, a state not already accepting jurisdiction under the optional clause might be encouraged to accept jurisdiction if a national were selected as a judge.

B. Ad Hoc Judges

A judge is not disqualified from hearing cases in which his own state is a party. Furthermore, if a party to a case does not have one of its nationals already on the court, that party may choose a person to sit as an *ad hoc* judge. *Ad hoc* judges have a full vote on the Court for matters pertaining to the case for which they were appointed. The Court, however, should be viewed as an unbiased body whose judges are independent of the state of their nationality. The system of *ad hoc* judges is inconsistent with this view and reinforces the perception that the Court is a political body whose judges represent their nations. Moreover, *ad hoc* judges do tend to be political and are more likely to support their state's position than are regular judges of the Court. The system of *ad hoc* judges is unnecessary and could be eliminated. The potential unfairness of one party but not the other having a national on the court could be overcome by allowing all parties one preemptory challenge to remove one judge from hearing the case. They could exercise this challenge to remove a judge who is a national of the opposing state or any other judge who they might believe is biased. If *ad hoc* judges are retained, in order to make them nonpolitical, they should be appointed by the Court rather than selected by the parties to the case.

V. JURISDICTION

The ICJ does not have jurisdiction to bring any state before it without that state's consent. Proposals advanced during the drafting of the PCIJ Statute, and again during the drafting of the ICJ Statute, to give the court compulsory jurisdiction over specified types of disputes or to allow entities other than nations to appear as parties were ultimately rejected. States may consent to the Court's jurisdiction in one of several ways. First, states may jointly agree to submit a pending dispute to the Court. Second, cases may be initiated by the unilateral filing of an application, provided that the respondent state has previously consented to jurisdiction through a provision to that effect in a treaty or by filing a declaration accepting the Court's jurisdiction under the "optional" clause. Where jurisdiction is based upon a treaty provision or the optional clause, general consent is given before the present dispute arises, and the respondent state may vigorously oppose having a particular conflict brought before the Court.

Only states may be parties to "contentious" cases. However, the Statute also grants the Court jurisdiction to issue advisory opinions upon the request of certain U.N. bodies. The statute does not provide for individuals or corporations to appear as parties in either contentious or advisory proceedings.

A. Special Agreements

Article 36(1) allows cases to be commenced by the joint filing of an agreement called a *compromis*. The *compromis* defines the issues that the Court is to address, and unlike cases founded upon other jurisdictional bases, the Court may not go any further even though other issues of international law are present. In a *compromis* both parties specifically consent to the instant dispute being heard by the Court, and consequently, such cases are seldom troubled by the problems of nonappearance or refusal to comply with judgments that often plague cases where unwilling litigants are brought before the Court. As a result, the Court has been much more successful in resolving disputes that are submitted pursuant to a *compromis* than in other cases.[51]

B. Treaties & Conventions

Jurisdiction may be conferred upon the Court by provisions, known as compromissory clauses, in treaties and international conventions. Approximately 750 treaties and conventions confer jurisdiction upon the ICJ (including about 500 treaties that formerly provided for

---

51/ There is an important difference in cases submitted pursuant to a *compromis* under U.S. law. A *compromis* is a treaty that requires ratification by the Senate before it can become effective. Because the Senate has already ratified treaties containing clauses providing for Court resolution of disputes (and until it was withdrawn, the U.S. acceptance of the optional clause) further consent is not required before a case is heard pursuant to the provisions of such treaties.

resolution by the PCIJ). The U.S. is a party to about 70 of these treaties and conventions,[52] which are of many different types. Many bilateral treaties, including most Friendship, Commerce & Navigation (FCN) treaties to which the U.S. is a party, contain compromissory clauses. The provision that was contained in the treaty with Nicaragua is typical:

> Any dispute between the Parties as to the interpretation or application of the present Treaty, not satisfactorily adjusted by diplomacy, shall be submitted to the International Court of Justice, unless the Parties agree to settlement by some other pacific means. (Article XXIV(2))

> [T]he jurisdiction of the International Court of Justice at the Hague as regards the interpretation and implementation of agreements on human rights should be binding on all states.
>
> *Soviet President Mikhail Gorbachev*
> *Address to the U.N. (December, 1988)*

Compromissory clauses are contained in a number of multilateral legislative conventions which establish rules of international law dealing with areas as diverse as narcotics trafficking, diplomatic relations, copyrights, and refugees. Recourse to the ICJ is also provided for in a number of treaties establishing international organizations, but not the U.N. Charter (other than advisory jurisdiction). In some cases these provisions permit the Court to act in essentially an appellate capacity, by reviewing the legality of the actions of the organizations. Article 75 of the Constitution of the World Health Organization is a typical provision:

> Any question or dispute concerning the interpretation or application of this Constitution which is not settled by negotiation or by the Health Assembly shall be referred to the International Court of Justice in conformity with the Statute of the Court, unless the parties agree on another mode of settlement.

Some compromissory clauses cover virtually all disputes under the applicable treaty while others are limited to specified issues. Parties are always free to agree to another dispute settlement mechanism, and compromissory clauses often require that parties exhaust other means of settlement before resorting to the ICJ. Some clauses are merely suggestive, providing for adjudication *only* if both parties subsequently agree.

While compromissory clauses usually provide for the settlement of disputes involving the treaty of which they are a party, a different approach is taken in the General Act for the Pacific Settlement of International Disputes.[53] Nineteen states, not including the U.S., are parties to this convention which deals generally with the peaceful settlement of disputes and provides for the submission of all controversies to the Court if they cannot be settled by other means:

> All disputes with regard to which the parties are in conflict as to their respective rights shall, subject to any reservations . . . , be submitted for decision to the Permanent Court of International Justice, unless the parties agree . . . to have resort to an arbitral tribunal.

52/ For a more detailed examination of compromissory clauses see F. Morrison, *Treaties as a Source of Jurisdiction, Especially in U.S. Practice*, in CROSSROADS, *supra* note 23, at 58. The appendices to that article list the treaties to which the U.S. is a party that contain compromissory clauses.

53/ 93 L.N.T.S. 343, Art. 17. The convention was adopted by the League Assembly on September 26, 1928.

Resolving Jurisdictional Disputes. Proceedings involving jurisdiction based upon compromissory clauses, as well as upon the optional clause described below, are commenced by the unilateral filing of an application with the Court. If jurisdiction is contested, the Court will hold a hearing and decide whether jurisdiction exists before proceeding to the merits of the case. States have a right not to be brought to Court without their consent. On the other hand, a state has a right to bring a case to the ICJ if consent is present. It is important that a decision on jurisdiction be made as soon as possible in order to avoid subjecting a state that has not consented to jurisdiction to unnecessary litigation costs or unwanted publicity. But jurisdictional questions are frequently bound up with the merits of the dispute, and no action should be taken at the preliminary stage that would prejudge the merits. For example, both the question of jurisdiction and the merits of a dispute may turn on whether certain conduct is covered by the treaty in question—if it is covered by the treaty there is jurisdiction and if it is not covered there is no jurisdiction. The Court has tended to take a middle ground between accepting mere allegations that jurisdiction exists and requiring proof that it is present.[54] Generally, the jurisdictional allegations must at least be plausible. In some cases, the question of jurisdiction cannot be determined at the preliminary stage and will be deferred until the merits phase. It is not unknown for the Court to decide that it has jurisdiction at a preliminary stage and change its mind after considering the merits of the case.[55]

Jurisdiction in the *Nicaragua* case was based in part upon the FCN treaty. Nicaragua argued that U.S. actions violated its obligations under the treaty to guarantee the freedom of each country's nationals to engage in commerce and navigation. The U.S. contested jurisdiction on the ground that the treaty only applied to the freedom of one state's citizens to engage in commercial activities in the other country, and that it did not apply to alleged military activities. The ICJ construed the scope to the FCN treaty broadly. All of the judges except Judges Ruda and Schwebel agreed with Nicaragua that the conduct alleged fell within the scope of the treaty.[56] The Court concluded that the compromissory clause would apply if the treaty covered any activity that had been disrupted by the military activities.[57]

54/ For a detailed discussion of how the Court has addressed jurisdictional issues under compromissory clauses see J. Charney, *Compromissory Clauses & the Jurisdiction of the International Court of Justice*, 81 AM. J. INT'L L. 855 (1987).

55/ In *Barcelona Traction*, the Court found jurisdiction at the preliminary objections phase, but at the merits phase it found that the applicant did not have standing and dismissed the case. *Barcelona Traction, Light & Power Co.* (Belg. v. Spain), 1964 I.C.J. 6 (preliminary); 1970 I.C.J. 3 (merits). The Court's Rules provide that if the jurisdictional issue "does not possess . . . an exclusively preliminary character," the Court must defer it until the merits phase. Rules, Art. 79(7).

56/ Judge Ruda made no determination on whether the alleged conduct fell within the scope of the treaty. He concluded that jurisdiction was lacking because Nicaragua had not attempted to negotiate a settlement before resorting to the Court, as required by the FCN treaty. The majority of the Court found that because Nicaragua had unsuccessfully negotiated with respect to its claim that the U.S. had violated international law, it would accomplish nothing to require it to negotiate the same issues with respect to the FCN treaty. 1984 I.C.J. at 452—54. Judge Schwebel found that jurisdiction was lacking because (1) Nicaragua had failed to rely on the treaty in its initial application, (2) Nicaragua had failed to exhaust its diplomatic remedies, and (3) the treaty did not cover the conduct alleged in the case. *Id.* at 638—37. In the *Hostages* case, the Court made clear that negotiations need not be resorted to where it is clear that they would be useless.

57/ Nicaragua did not include the FCN treaty in its initial application with the Court, but raised it for the first time in a later submission. The U.S. argued that all bases for jurisdiction must be set out in the application, (Cont'd)

C. The Optional Clause

States may confer general jurisdiction on the Court pursuant to Article 36(2), often referred to as the optional clause.[58] This clause permits states to file unilateral declarations accepting the Court's jurisdiction in regard to disputes with other nations that have filed similar declarations. These declarations can encompass any legal dispute.[59] Declarations pursuant to the optional clause may also include reservations that limit their scope. In determining whether it has jurisdiction, the court applies the principle of reciprocity. It has jurisdiction only if the dispute is within the scope of both that applicant and respondent states' declarations. Thus, a respondent state may invoke not only the reservations in its own declaration, but the reservations in the applicant's declaration as well.

When the Statute of the PCIJ was adopted, the optional clause was expected to constitute the Court's principal source of jurisdiction. This was not to be. In only about one-third of all contentious cases brought to the Court was the jurisdictional claim based on the optional clause, and in a number of these the Court found jurisdiction lacking. The small number of cases filed under the optional clause is attributable in part to the reluctance of states to submit declarations accepting the Court's jurisdiction. In 1939, 40 of the 52 states that were parties to the PCIJ Statute (77%) had accepted jurisdiction under the optional clause. Today, only 57 out of 185 states that are parties to the Court's Statute (31%) accept the ICJ's general jurisdiction. Of the five permanent members of the Security Council, currently only the U.K. has an active declaration under the optional clause.

Moreover, few if the states accepting the ICJ's general jurisdiction do so unconditionally and without reservations. Of those declarations containing reservations, some reservations are so minor as to narrow the Court's jurisdiction little, if at all, while others are so broad as to make the declaration virtually meaningless. Reservations contain widely varying terms. In interpreting the scope of a reservation, the Court attempts to discern what the intent was of the state when making its declaration. This is different from interpreting the meaning of treaty provisions where there is generally the record of the negotiations. Moreover, two different reservations having the same language may, in theory, have different meanings based upon different intents by the states making them. As a result, it is difficult for a state to know the construction that the Court will place on its, or another state's, declaration.

57/ (Cont'd)
and that Nicaragua should not be allowed to amend its allegations to add this alternative basis for jurisdiction. The Court, while noting that it would have been better practice for Nicaragua to have included this allegation in its application, found that there was no good reason for preventing it from adding it later. This is certainly reasonable. Nothing would have been accomplished by denying jurisdiction on this ground since Nicaragua could simply have filed a new application based upon the FCN treaty. The U.S. did not take action to terminate the FCN treaty until May 1985 (to be effective one year later).

58/ The jurisdiction conferred by the optional clause is frequently referred to as "compulsory jurisdiction." This term is misleading since jurisdiction under a compromissory clause is equally compulsory. This monograph will use the term "general jurisdiction" instead.

59/ Jurisdiction under Article 36(2) may encompass (a) the interpretation of treaties, (b) any question of international law, (c) facts upon which a violation of international law might depend, and (d) the reparation to be made for a violation of an international obligation.

1. Creation, Duration & Termination of Declarations

The *Nicaragua* case presented several interesting issues concerning the creation, modification, duration, and termination of declarations. The U.S. contended that Nicaragua lacked standing to bring the case under the optional clause because it had never submitted a valid declaration under that clause. Nicaragua relied upon Article 36(5), which provides that declarations under the PCIJ Statute shall be deemed acceptances of the jurisdiction of the ICJ. The facts surrounding Nicaragua's declaration, however, are unique. In 1929, Nicaragua signed the PCIJ Statute and made a declaration accepting the jurisdiction of the Court without reservation. However, the declaration would not become effective until Nicaragua ratified the PCIJ Statute and deposited the instruments of ratification with the League. Nicaragua's legislature completed ratification in 1935, and in 1939 Nicaragua sent a telegram notifying the League of the ratification and indicating that the instruments of ratification would follow. They were never received. Consequently, Nicaragua was not technically a party to the PCIJ statute at the time it became an original member of the U.N. in 1945. The U.S. maintained that because the declaration was never effective under the PCIJ, it could not become a valid declaration under the ICJ Statute. The Court accepted Nicaragua's contention that just as completing ratification of the PCIJ statute would have made its declaration effective, so too its ratification of the U.N. Charter and ICJ Statute perfected its declaration. In addition, Nicaragua had been listed in numerous Court Yearbooks and Reports as having accepted ICJ's jurisdiction under the optional clause, and it had never objected to being so included.[60] The Court found that Nicaragua's consistent acquiescence to being listed as accepting jurisdiction manifested its intent to recognize the jurisdiction of the Court—whether it appeared in a case as an applicant or a respondent.[61] This determination has proved controversial. While the Court might, under these unique circumstances, have ruled that Nicaragua had not filed a valid declaration, its determination that its declaration was valid was not unreasonable. Clearly, Nicaragua believed that its declaration was valid, otherwise it would have filed a new declaration shortly before, or contemporaneous with, its submission of the case to the Court.

Nicaragua also considered some important issues regarding the last minute attempt by the U.S. to modify its declaration. Three days prior to the filing of Nicaragua's application, the U.S. attempted to modify its declaration to exclude disputes involving Central America. The 1946 U.S. declaration, however, provided that it could be terminated upon six months notice. The Court found that the U.S. was bound by this notice provision with respect to its efforts to modify the declaration (otherwise it would be meaningless since the declaration could be "modified" away). The U.S. pointed out that the Nicaragua declaration was silent as to the notice necessary for termination or modification, and the U.S. argued that under these circumstances a notice of termination of the Nicaraguan declaration would be effective

60/ Evidence was conflicting. The U.S. cited several instances when officials of a previous Nicaraguan government asserted that Nicaragua did not consider itself to have accepted the Court's general jurisdiction. But, there was also evidence that the U.S. in several documents had listed Nicaragua as having filed a valid declaration.

61/ This was not the first case in which the ICJ examined a nation's conduct in determining whether it accepted the jurisdiction of the Court. In *Temple of Preah Vihear (Cambodia v. Thailand)*, 1961 I.C.J. 17, 34, the Court noted that Thailand's consistent attitude over many years was proof of its intention to submit itself to the general jurisdiction of the Court.

immediately. The U.S. maintained that under the principle of reciprocity, it could invoke the Nicaraguan declaration's termination provision to terminate the U.S. declaration with respect to Nicaragua upon notice. The Court did not accept this argument. It drew a distinction between reservations, which deal with the scope and substance of the commitments made in the declaration, and conditions pertaining to a declaration's creation, duration, and extinction. The Court found that reciprocity applied to reservations only, not to such conditions.[62] Moreover, it is well established that the jurisdiction of the Court is based upon the situation at the time it is seized with a case by the proper filing of an application. Therefore the fact that a declaration might be terminated after a case has been filed will not defeat jurisdiction that was present at the time of filing. Accordingly, the Court found that it had jurisdiction to entertain the case under the optional clause.

The ICJ's holding that conditions relating to the duration and termination of declarations are not subject to reciprocity is somewhat disturbing.[63] A large variety of such provisions have been included in declarations filed by states. Some declarations, like that of the U.S., provide that they may be terminated a specified time after notice is given while others may be terminated immediately upon notice. Several declarations are in effect for a specific term and may be terminated upon notice after expiration of that term, but others are extended automatically for a further fixed term if not withdrawn. Many, like Nicaragua's, contain no provision relating to termination. By declining to apply the principle of reciprocity to these provisions, the states are placed at a position of inequality before the Court. There is no incentive for a state to limit its right to terminate its declaration. Under these circumstances, states would be well advised to provide for termination upon notice. The Court is certainly correct, however, that there are fundamental differences between reservations and conditions pertaining to the modification and termination of declarations. These differences make the concept of reciprocity inappropriate with respect to conditions. The circumstances under which declarations can be modified or terminated should be uniform for all states, not dependent upon the contents of each state's declaration. Ideally, the Statute should be amended to provide uniform conditions under which declarations can be modified. Alternatively, given the difficulty of amending the Statute, the ICJ might accomplish this result through rulemaking.

2. Reservations

While a complete examination of the Court's treatment of declarations and their reservations is beyond the scope of this paper, an examination of some of the more important issues surrounding them may prove useful. Many reservations do not narrow appreciably, if

---

62/ The Court also rejected the U.S. argument that because the Nicaragua declaration was silent as to its termination, it could be terminated upon notice. The Court applied principles of treaty law to find that where a treaty is silent as to the rights of parties to terminate it, the treaty can be terminated upon reasonable notice. The Court did not define what notice would be "reasonable" for termination of a declaration under the optional clause, but it did find that the three days between the U.S. notice of modification of its declaration and the filing by Nicaragua of its application would not be reasonable.

63/ It also seems somewhat anomalous that a declaration that contains no provision regarding termination requires a reasonable notice, while a provision that explicitly provides for termination upon notice is apparently effective.

at all, the scope of the declaration. For example, most reservations explicitly require reciprocity even though that requirement is inherent in all proceedings based upon the optional clause. Other reservations seek to exclude matters where the parties have agreed to use another method to resolve the dispute. However, if the parties agree that a particular dispute should be settled in some other matter, it would never be filed with the Court in the first place, and if the dispute is covered by a treaty provision requiring some other method of settlement, the Court would most certainly hold the parties to their agreement to exhaust the other method of settlement.

Domestic Jurisdiction. Some reservations exclude matters that are exclusively within a state's domestic jurisdiction. This would seem unnecessary since the optional clause pertains only to disputes that have an international aspect, which would necessarily exclude matters that are *exclusively* within any state's domestic jurisdiction. Other declarations, however, exclude matters that are *essentially* within a state's domestic jurisdiction, and such provisions may limit somewhat the scope of a declaration. Prior to its termination by President Reagan in 1985, the U.S. declaration included what is known as the "Connally Reservation," which excluded "disputes with regard to matters which are essentially within the domestic jurisdiction of the United States of America *as determined by the United States of America.*"

The self-judging nature of the Connally Reservation proved controversial, since it seemed to confer on the U.S. the right to claim that any proceeding was within the scope of the reservation, even if the claim was made in bad faith. *Norwegian Loans*, a case initiated by France against Norway pertaining to whether certain loans were required to be repaid in Norwegian or French currency was the first case to apply such a reservation. The French declaration contained a reservation patterned after the Connally Reservation. The ICJ found that Norway was entitled to invoke the reservation contained in the French declaration and therefore found that it lacked jurisdiction. During the time that the U.S. declaration was in effect, the U.S. sought to invoke the Connally Reservation only once, in *Interhandel*. That case, which was brought by Switzerland, concerned shares of a Swiss company that the U.S. had seized during World War II pursuant to the Trading with the Enemy Act. The ICJ dismissed the case on the ground that Switzerland had failed to exhaust its local remedies before resorting to the Court, and therefore did not have to address the issues raised by the reservation directly. Judge Lauterpacht in a separate opinion, however, reiterated a position he had espoused in *Norwegian Loans*—that the self-judging reservation nullified the U.S. declaration. Judge Lauterpacht found the reservation contrary to Article 36(6) which gives the Court the power to decide whether it has jurisdiction. He also found that the reservation made the declaration meaningless, since conferral upon the U.S. of the right to determine whether jurisdiction is present deprived the declaration of the character of a legal instrument that expressed legal rights and obligations.[64]

The Connally Reservation was next an issue in the *Bulgarian Aerial Incident* case which concerned the downing over Bulgarian territory of an Israeli civil aircraft having U.S. nationals on board. Bulgaria invoked the Connally Reservation in the U.S. declaration. The State Department Legal Advisor initially argued that the Connally Reservation was governed by a

---

64/ Judge Klaestad argued that the Connally Reservation was invalid and severable from the rest of the U.S. declaration. Judge Lauterpacht rejected this argument by noting that the reservation had been essential for ratification of the declaration.

rule of reasonable interpretation and could therefore be invoked only in good faith. However, he was summoned before the Senate Committee on Foreign Relations and told that invocation of the reservation was intended to be at the complete discretion of the U.S. or the other parties. The State Department then formally repudiated the argument that the reservation must be reasonably interpreted, and withdrew the case stating that it considered mere invocation of the reservation to be a bar to jurisdiction. It is to the credit of the U.S. that the it did not invoke the reservation to defeat jurisdiction in the *Nicaragua* proceeding.

To permit states to judge for themselves whether a reservation applies is contrary to the spirit of the optional clause. Moreover, the Connally Reservation was of questionable value to the U.S. The reservation virtually assured that the U.S. would fail whenever it sought to bring a case against an unwilling adversary, because the respondent could invoke it under the principle of reciprocity. It most certainly inhibited the filing of a number of applications where it was clear that the other side would invoke the reservation if the application were filed. The reservation therefore limited substantially the opportunities for the U.S. to be a plaintiff, without providing significant protection to actual U.S. interests.

Multilateral Treaties. The former U.S. declaration also included the "Vandenberg Reservation" that excluded "disputes arising under a multilateral treaty, unless . . . all parties to the treaty affected by the decision are also parties to the case before the Court . . . ."[65] In *Nicaragua*, the Court deferred consideration of this reservation until the merits phase. There, the ICJ found that the reservation barred the Nicaraguan claim in so far as it was based upon multilateral treaties, including the U.N. Charter and the Charter of the OAS. The ICJ found, however, that this did not prevent it from considering whether the U.S. had violated customary international law, even where evidence of what constitutes customary law was obtained from U.N. resolutions. In this regard there is substantial overlap between customary international law and U.N. resolutions (which, in theory, cannot make law but may be a guide to what the law is).

One purpose of the Vandenberg Reservation was to ensure that any decision that binds the U.S. also binds the other parties to the treaty. It was feared that the other parties to the treaty might contend that the judgment does not bind them, and that this would place the U.S. at a disadvantage. This concern seems unwarranted. A judgment in a particular proceeding would bind the U.S. only with respect to that specific dispute. It would not strictly bind the U.S. with respect to similar disputes with either the same party or with other parties to the treaty. Moreover, the precedential effect of a case would apply to all nations equally, irrespective of whether they were parties to the case. It is difficult therefore to see how the Vandenberg Reservation protected any significant U.S. interest.[66]

Furthermore, to the extent that the ICJ can base its decision on customary international law, as it did in *Nicaragua,* the reservation does not appreciably limit a country's exposure to

---

65/ This language is ambiguous. The U.S. interpreted this provision in the *Nicaragua* case to require the presence of the states affected by the dispute, but some states having similar reservations interpret them to require the presence of all parties to the treaty.

66/ Some of the concerns underlying the Vandenberg Reservation apply to multilateral disputes generally, whether or not they are based upon a multilateral treaty. *See* Part IX, *infra.* A reservation dealing with all multilateral disputes generally would be the appropriate way to deal with such disputes.

liability, but it may limit unreasonably the law that the Court can apply, since it may require the Court to ignore law that is based upon multilateral treaties. This might distort the law in a manner not necessarily to the advantage of the party invoking the reservation.[67]

Other Reservations. Nations may bring cases against other countries immediately upon filing a declaration accepting the Court's general jurisdiction. This may arguably lead to an inequity if a nation accepts the Court's jurisdiction primarily for the purpose of bringing a particular case. For example, three days after Portugal filed its declaration, it instituted a proceeding against India concerning the right of transit to Portuguese enclaves within India.[68] The Court held that the short time period between depositing the declaration and bringing the case did not deprive it of jurisdiction. One popular type of reservation is intended to protect a state from such tactics. Such reservations may take the form of excluding cases where the plaintiff has accepted jurisdiction only for the purpose of the particular dispute or where the plaintiff has accepted jurisdiction less than a specified time before bringing the case.[69]

Some declarations include reservations designed to exclude specific categories of disputes. For example, in 1970 Canada proclaimed a marine anti-pollution zone and made a new declaration that excluded disputes relating to pollution within this zone. Canada removed this reservation in 1985. Several exclude disputes involving armed hostilities. Other reservations exclude disputes with particular states. In this respect, some members of the British Commonwealth exclude disputes with other Commonwealth members and some states exclude disputes involving states with which they do not have diplomatic relations. The 1984 modification of the U.S. declaration, to exclude disputes with Central American nations, made in an attempt to head off the Nicaraguan application, is another example.

D. Advisory Jurisdiction

Only states, and not individuals or international organizations can be parties under the ICJ's contentious jurisdiction. However, Article 96 of the U.N. Charter and Article 65 of the

---

67/ For example, a state might have a certain right under customary international law, but this right might be restricted or expanded by a multilateral convention. Is it reasonable under such circumstances for the Court to decide the case based solely upon customary law, while ignoring treaty provisions that modify that law? But if the Court takes into account the treaty provisions, would it not be ignoring the multilateral treaty reservation? This practical difficulty of separating customary and multilateral treaty law was a major source of criticism of the ICJ's determination that it could base its judgment in *Nicaragua* on customary international law without violating the Vandenberg Reservation. On the other hand, any multilateral treaty reservation that includes the U.N. Charter would severely restrict the scope of the declaration.

68/ *Right of Passage Over Indian Territory*, 1960 I.C.J. 6. Although Portugal applied for U.N. membership in 1946, it was not admitted until December 14, 1955. It had not sought to become a party to the Statute of the Court before it was admitted to the U.N. Five days later, on December 19, it filed its declaration under the optional clause. It filed its application commencing the proceeding on December 22.

69/ The U.S. declaration did not contain such a reservation. Thus, the controversy in the Nicaragua case over whether Nicaragua had accepted the Court's jurisdiction could have been obviated had Nicaragua filed a declaration at the time it brought suit against the U.S. clarifying that it accepted jurisdiction.

Statute allow the Court to give advisory opinions at the request of the General Assembly, the Security Council, or other organs of the U.N. and its specialized agencies that are so authorized by the General Assembly.[70] The ICJ has issued advisory opinions dealing with such diverse issues as South Africa's administration of South West Africa, the admission of new members to the U.N., the obligation to pay for peacekeeping operations, the discharge of U.N. employees, and the interpretation of treaties.

> One should not forget the capacities of the International Court. . . . The General Assembly and the Security Council could approach it more often for consultative conclusions on international disputes. Its mandatory jurisdiction should be organized by all on mutually agreed-upon conditions. We are convinced that a comprehensive system of security is, at the same time, a system of universal law and order ensuring the primacy of international law in politics.
>
> *Soviet President Mikhail Gorbachev*
> *"The Reality and Guarantees of a Secure World"*
> *(September 17, 1987)*

Advisory and contentious proceedings have important differences. First, only international organizations can request advisory opinions while the parties to contentious proceedings are states. Second, judgments in contentious cases are binding on the parties while advisory opinions are not. This may be a difference more in theory than in practice. The lack of an effective enforcement mechanism makes binding judgments illusory and there may be substantial pressure to comply with advisory opinions. Advisory opinions are intended primarily to resolve questions of law, not to resolve disputes concerning the facts underlying the matter, but the presence of a factual issue does not prevent the Court from issuing an advisory opinion.[71] Like contentious proceedings, advisory proceedings may relate to actual disputes between states. Interested states have a right to participate in the proceedings, but it is more limited than it would be in a contentious case. Unlike contentious cases, parties with an interest in an advisory proceeding need not have consented to jurisdiction.[72] Article 68 states that the ICJ shall be guided by the provisions in the Statute pertaining to contentious proceedings. Pursuant to this

---

70/ Strictly speaking, the General Assembly and Security Council are allowed to request advisory opinions on any legal question, while other organs are limited to opinions on legal questions arising within the scope of their activities. This has not proved to be an important distinction. The Court has taken a broad view of what is within the scope of an organ's activities.

The General Assembly has conferred authority to request advisory opinions on the following U.N. organs: Economic and Social Council, Trusteeship Council, Interim Committee of the General Assembly, and the Committee on Applications for Review of Administrative Tribunal Judgments. The following specialized agencies are also authorized to request advisory opinions: ILO, Food and Agriculture Organization, UNESCO, International Civil Aviation Organization, WHO, World Bank, IMF, International Finance Corp., International Development Association, International Telecommunications Union, World Meteorological Organization, International Maritime Organization, World Intellectual Property Organization, International Fund for Agricultural Development, U.N. Industrial Development Organization, and the International Atomic Energy Agency.

71/ *See, e.g., Western Sahara*, 1975 I.C.J. 12 at ¶ 17.

72/ *Id.* ¶ 30.

provision, where an advisory proceeding pertains to an actual dispute between states, the Court even applies the provisions relating to *ad hoc* judges.

1. Appeals from Administrative Tribunals

While, in theory, the ICJ is limited to giving advisory opinions to international organizations, a method has evolved to broaden this jurisdiction so that it may in effect hear appeals from administrative tribunals, where the actual parties in interest may be a state or individual as well as the international organization. The U.N. Administrative Tribunal (UNAT) is an organ created by the General Assembly that is charged with hearing appeals from U.N. employees concerning personnel matters. An advisory opinion issued in 1954 dealt with whether the General Assembly was required to comply with awards made by the UNAT.[73] That dispute concerned several U.S. nationals who had been fired from their jobs at the behest of the U.S., because the U.S. believed they had communist leanings. The U.S. opposed the UNAT award of severance pay. The U.S. contended that the General Assembly as a principal organ was not required to carry out the award of the UNAT, a subsidiary organ. The ICJ found that the UNAT was an independent and truly judicial body. The ICJ held that since the UNAT's judgments were under its statute final and without appeal, the organization became legally bound. The Court noted, however, that the General Assembly could amend the Tribunal's statute to provide expressly for appeals, but it ruled out any review by the General Assembly because it could hardly act as a judicial organ.

In response to the 1954 opinion, the General Assembly amended the UNAT's statute to provide a mechanism for appeal. The Secretary General, any state, or the individual concerned may request review of the Tribunal's judgment by the Committee on Applications for Review of Judgments of the Administrative Tribunal. If the Committee decides that there is a substantial basis for the Appeal, it may request an advisory opinion from the ICJ. Thus, individuals can obtain indirect access to the Court. There is a similar mechanism for obtaining review of judgments by the ILO Administrative Tribunal. Other international organizations may use either of these administrative tribunals and take advantage of their review mechanisms.

This mechanism for reviewing administrative decisions is an imperfect substitute for direct appeals to the Court by aggrieved parties, which is not possible under the current Statute. The ICJ was not designed to be an appellate court. Consequently, its role in this regard has been criticized as exceeding its authority under its Statute and because its procedures are not appropriate for what are essentially contentious proceedings between individuals and international organizations. Nonetheless, there is no reason why the Court should not respond to requests for advisory opinions that review the findings of another tribunal even if this function was not contemplated when the Statute was drafted. The procedures for UNAT review, however, are open to criticism. While the Committee is necessary to screen out frivolous complaints, it may be screening out too many since only a small fraction of requests submitted to it have resulted in requests for advisory opinions. This may indicate that the Committee is acting politically. Moreover, the scope of review is limited to questions of law, jurisdiction, and procedure; factual matters cannot be appealed. Procedurally, individuals are placed in a position of inequality before the Court, because the Statute and rules contemplate

---

73/ *Effect of Award of Compensation Made by the UNAT*, 1954 I.C.J. 47 (July 13).

participation by states and organizations but not by individuals. Perhaps the major problem with the ICJ hearing appeals from administrative tribunals is that the judges on the Court have expertise in general international law and not in personnel matters. Judge Ago, for example, suggests that it would be best to create a new court specifically to hear appeals from such administrative tribunals.[74]

2. Making Advisory Opinions Binding

One important aspect of the Statutes of the U.N. and ILO administrative tribunals is that they both provide that advisory opinions of the Court shall be treated by the parties as conclusive. This gives the ICJ's advisory opinions a binding character that is nominally inconsistent with the notion of an "advisory" opinion. The Court has found no problem with this treatment. The ICJ has noted that (1) the task of the Court does not vary with whether the provision under which the request was submitted provides that the opinion will be binding, (2) the procedures of the Court and form of the opinion are the same as other advisory proceedings, (3) the binding nature of the opinion arises from provisions unrelated to those which govern the activities of the Court, and (4) the binding nature of the opinion is only a rule of conduct for the parties to the dispute.

A number of other multilateral conventions also contain provisions making advisory opinions binding upon the parties. These conventions include the Convention on the Privileges and Immunities of the United Nations, the Vienna Convention on the Law of Treaties between States and International Organizations or between International Organizations, and the U.N. Convention against Illicit Traffic in Narcotic Drugs and Psychotropic Substances. Provisions making advisory opinions binding provide a method for greatly expanding the jurisdiction of the Court. Such provisions are not, however, without difficulties. Judge Ago has argued that in view of the inappropriateness of the Court's procedures with respect to such advisory proceedings, it would be desirable to amend the Court's Statute to give the ICJ explicit authority to conduct contentions proceedings that involve international organizations.[75]

E. Proposals to Enhance the ICJ's Jurisdiction

Most proposals to revitalize the ICJ focus on the Court's jurisdictional scheme. Antiquated concepts of international law underlie many of the statute's jurisdictional provisions. Thus, the limitation on contentious cases to disputes between nations was based upon the notion that international law governs only states, not individuals or even international organizations. Ideas concerning sovereignty form the basis of the Statute's requirement that states can only be brought before the Court with their consent. These concepts are gradually changing, but there is likely to be substantial resistance from many parts of the world community to radical

---

74/ R. Ago, *"Binding" Advisory Opinions of the ICJ*, AM. J. INT'L L., 439, 444—45 (1991). Another alternative would be for the ICJ to create a chamber to hear such cases.

75/ *Id.* at 450—51.

changes to the Court's jurisdiction. Nonetheless, more modest jurisdictional enhancements might be attainable. Some of the proposals set forth below would require amendment of the Statute, while others might be accomplished more easily.

1. Expanding Access to International Organizations

The ability of international organizations to obtain advisory opinions concerning the scope of their activities should be enhanced. Under the Charter, the General Assembly may authorize only other organs of the U.N. and its specialized agencies to request advisory opinions. This should be expanded to include all public international organizations, including NATO and regional organizations such as the OAS or the OAU. Additionally, the Statute might be amended to eliminate the requirement of General Assembly authorization entirely.

The General Assembly should also take steps under the current statute to broaden access to the ICJ's advisory jurisdiction. It should grant additional bodies authorization to seek advisory opinions. These authorizations should include the Secretary General. Advisory opinions should prove to be an effective tool in his efforts to mediate disputes between member states and could assist in resolving legal disputes concerning his authority. It can be difficult for either the General Assembly or the Security Council to muster the necessary votes to request an advisory opinion, even in pressing cases. As a single individual, the Secretary General could request opinions on his own initiative without any undue delay. For this same reason, however, many nations will be reluctant to grant him sole authority to request advisory opinions that might embarrass them in the future. It may therefore be necessary to strictly limit the circumstances under which the Secretary General can request opinions. The U.S. Commission on Improving the Effectiveness of the U.N., for example, proposes that he be granted authority to request advisory opinions in cases where both parties to a dispute have asked him to mediate.

The General Assembly should set up a mechanism by which advisory opinions may be obtained by organizations that are not yet authorized to seek opinions. The system used for obtaining review of administrative tribunal decisions could serve as a model. A screening committee should be set up with authority to refer requests from organizations to the Court. Its authority should extend to forwarding requests from certain non-governmental organizations such as the International Committee of the Red Cross.

Organizations already having the authority to request advisory opinions should be encouraged to make greater use of this authority,[76] and it should be made easier for them to request opinions. Certainly, the ICJ should not be asked to issue an opinion on frivolous matters or upon the request of only a few states. Nonetheless, advisory opinions should be available upon the request of a substantial minority of the members of the organization where a real and significant dispute exists. A minority (e.g. 30—40 percent) of the members of an

---

76/ The 1976 State Department Report indicated that some organizations may be reluctant to use the ICJ because the Court is unfamiliar with the organizations's activities and might not be sensitive to their internal requirements. The report noted that one solution would be for the Court to make greater use of assessors and experts or to refer such cases to a chamber with expertise in the organization's activities. *See also* L. Gross, *The International Ct. of Justice: Consideration of Requirements for Enhancing its Role in the International Legal Order,* 65 AM. J. INT'L L. (1971).

organization or of a screening committee should be sufficient to request an advisory opinion. Accordingly, it is recommended that international organizations amend their charters to permit a specified minority to request an advisory opinion.[77]

The ICJ's Statute should also be expanded to permit the U.N. and other international institutions to appear as parties to contentious cases both against states and other organizations. The ICJ's second advisory opinion, *Reparation for Injuries Suffered in the Service of the U.N.*,[78] dealt with whether the U.N. has the capacity to bring claims for injuries sustained by U.N. personnel in the line of duty against a government responsible for those injuries. The Court found that the U.N. possesses international personality that gives it the capacity to make such claims both on behalf of itself and on behalf of injured individuals. Thus, while the U.N.'s capacity has been established to assert claims against nations, it has no right to adjudicate such claims through the Court. Although the ability of an international organization to seek advisory opinions can be useful in settling disputes with member states or other international organizations, it can never serve as a full substitute for contentious jurisdiction. One of the justifications given by South Africa for not complying with the Court's advisory opinions concerning its administration of Southwest Africa was that the opinions were not binding!

Domestic courts serve to resolve disputes not only between individuals, but also between individuals and the state itself. This permits individuals to challenge state action through the judicial process. There is no comparable way for states to challenge the legality of U.N. actions. For example, the cornerstone of the U.N. system is the Security Council's authority to make decisions binding on all members under Chapter VII. However, states have given the Council the power to make binding decisions only in cases where there is a "threat to the peace, breach of the peace, or act of aggression." A serious constitutional crisis could result if a member state should claim that a Security Council resolution is invalid because it exceeds the Council's authority and if there is no way to resolve the dispute.[79] The *Lockerbie* case is illustrative. The U.S. and the U.K. sought Security Council action to compel Libya to extradite two Libyans accused of the destruction of a U.S. aircraft above Lockerbie, Scotland. Because Libya could not directly challenge the Security Council action, it sought to block Council action indirectly by instituting Court proceedings against the U.S. and the U.K., seeking to enjoin them from attempting to compel Libya to turn over the accused. While this attempt to use the ICJ to block the U.S. and the U.K. from taking their disputes to the Security Council is questionable, it was the only method by which Libya could challenge the Council action. The ICJ denied Libya's request for preliminary measures primarily because it felt constrained to apply the Security Council resolution. Nonetheless, several judges indicated that the Security Council's authority is not unlimited, but they did not indicate how those limits should be determined. Judge Shahabuddeen stated in this regard:

77/ This is similar to the U.S. Supreme Court which must select only a small minority of the cases submitted to it to hear. An affirmative vote of only four of its nine justices is required for the Court to consider a case.

78/ 1949 I.C.J. 174.

79/ W. Reisman, *The Constitutional Crisis in the United Nations*, 87 AM. J. INT'L L. 83 (1993). The breakup of the Soviet Union provides another illustration of a possible challenge to Security Council action. A state might argue that Russia is not a proper successor to the Soviet Union and a decision in which Russia participated is not valid because the Council is improperly constituted.

> The question . . . is whether a decision of the Security Council may override the legal rights of States, and, if so, whether there are any limitations on the power of the Council to characterize a situation as one justifying the making of a decision entailing such consequences. . . . [I]s there any conceivable point beyond which a legal issue may properly arise as to the competence of the Security Council to produce such overriding results? If there are limits, what are those limits and what body . . . is competent to say what those limits are?
>
> If the answers to these delicate and complex questions are all in the negative, the position is potentially curious. It would not, on that account be necessarily unsustainable in law; and how far the Court can enter the field is another matter.[80]

The Statute could be amended to permit international organizations to confer jurisdiction on the court in a similar manner as currently provided for by the Statute. Compromissory clauses that specify the circumstances under which an international organization could sue or be sued could be included in the organization's constitutional document or in supplemental treaties. Jurisdiction could also be conferred through special agreements. A separate provision might be included in the ICJ Statute to specify the circumstances under which the Court would have jurisdiction over litigation between the U.N. and other international organizations.[81] Where an organization has multiple organs, such as the U.N., consideration must be given to which organs would have authority to commence a case. The State Department in its 1976 Report endorsed the concept of contentious jurisdiction for international organizations, and because of the potentially serious consequences of litigation it recommended that both the Council and the Assembly should concur in initiating litigation involving the U.N.

2. Encouraging Greater Use by States

The key to greater use of the Court is to convince States that the peaceful resolution of disputes according to the law is in everyone's interest. States should be encouraged to utilize the ICJ to a greater degree. The U.S. should demonstrate its support for the Court and the rule of law by reaccepting jurisdiction under the optional clause without attaching debilitating reservations such as the Connally reservation.[82] If the U.S. leads by example, other states may follow by also accepting the Court's general jurisdiction. Amendment of the Statute to

---

80/ *Lockerbie*, 1992 I.C.J. 114, 142 (Shahabuddeen, J.).

81/ Some have suggested that organizations could file declarations under the optional clause. This is not likely to be useful. In nearly all cases, states involved in litigation with international organizations would be members of the organization. The most effective way to provide jurisdiction in such cases would be through a compromissory clause in the organization's charter.

82/ A specific proposal for a declaration accepting jurisdiction is set forth in L. Sohn, *Suggestions for the Limited Acceptance of Compulsory Jurisdiction of the ICJ by the U.S.*, 18 GA. J. INT'L & COMP. L 1 (1988). This particular proposal contains more extensive reservations than are desirable, but they may be necessary in order to obtain Senate ratification. The reservations include (1) domestic jurisdiction (but without the self-judging provision of the Connally reservation), (2) disputes relating to any question affecting the national security of the U.S. or any state party to a collective security agreement with the U.S., and (3) multilateral treaties.

provide true compulsory jurisdiction, whereby the ICJ would have jurisdiction over all disputes between states without the necessity that they first consent to jurisdiction would also be highly desirable; but such a move is unlikely to gain sufficient support from the world community for many years.[83]

> [T]he time has come for mankind to make the role of law in international affairs as normal as it is now in domestic affairs. . . . [O]ne will sometimes lose as well as win. But nations can endure and accept an adverse decision rendered by competent and impartial tribunals. In hundreds of arbitral and judicial decisions over the past 170 years, it has been almost unheard of for one of the parties to refuse to comply with the decision . . . . This is so, I believe, for one good reason: if an international conflict leads to armed conflict, everyone loses, if armed conflict is avoided, everyone wins. It is better to lose a point now and then in an international tribunal and gain a world in which everyone lives at peace under the rule of law.
>
> *President Dwight D. Eisenhower*
> *Address to University of Delhi*
> *(December 11, 1959)*

A general dispute settlement convention might be more effective than the optional clause in establishing general jurisdiction. Like the optional clause, it would provide for compulsory jurisdiction between parties to the convention. Such a convention would provide a degree of uniformity that is lacking in the patchwork of declarations submitted under the optional clause. It would include limitations commonly contained in reservations under the optional clause, and would prohibit further reservations. However, such a convention could be drafted to provide a menu of types of disputes that a state might wish to include or exclude. Unlike the optional clause, a convention would provide uniform provisions with respect to joining and withdrawing from the convention. Another advantage is that it may be easier to construe the terms of a negotiated convention than it is to construe the intent underlying a unilateral declaration. An alternative to a general dispute settlement convention would be a series of narrowly drawn treaties conferring jurisdiction on the Court over a single type of dispute, e.g. over human rights issues or boundary disputes.

In addition, newly negotiated treaties should contain compromissory clauses that include judicial resolution of disputes. Establishment of costly new methods of resolving disputes should be avoided when the ICJ could serve as well. For example, the Law of the Sea Convention permits parties to elect among several dispute settlement methods, including arbitration and judicial settlement by the ICJ. The parties can also choose a new tribunal created by the Convention. The Law of the Sea Tribunal was created, in part, because a number of states distrusted the ICJ and because a tribunal was wanted with expertise in the law of the sea. The statute of this new tribunal is to a substantial extent based upon the ICJ Statute. It is difficult to envision how the resulting tribunal will be more satisfactory to the states that were dissatisfied with the ICJ. To the extent that they were unhappy with certain

---

83/ Another possibility (which was considered when the PCIJ Statute was drafted) would be to modify the optional clause to make jurisdiction compulsory unless nations make a specific reservation to jurisdiction. This would reverse the present procedure by placing the onus on states that wish to opt out of compulsory jurisdiction, and it could lead to more states being subject to the ICJ's jurisdiction.

ICJ judges, the makeup of the Court will change over time and there is no reason to believe that the judges elected to the law of the sea tribunal will prove more satisfactory to those states. In addition, law of the sea issues could be adjudicated by a chamber of the ICJ with expertise in that subject. While establishment of the Law of the Sea Tribunal may be justified as necessary to obtain wide acceptance of the convention, maintenance of the tribunal will be costly and there is no reason to believe that it will be able to resolve disputes more fairly or expeditiously than the ICJ.

3. Allowing Access by Domestic Courts

A number of commentators have quite reasonably proposed that domestic courts should be permitted to request advisory opinions on questions of international law relevant to cases pending before them.[84] The Court of Justice of the European Community is frequently used as a model. The Treaty of Rome provides that the Court of Justice may issue advisory opinions on questions concerning the interpretation of the Treaty of Rome or actions and regulations issued pursuant to the Treaty. Such advisory opinions may be requested by any court of a member state if it is relevant to the case and *must* be requested if the case is pending in a court from which there is no appeal.[85] Under most current proposals for the ICJ, no domestic court would be required to seek an advisory opinion and requests would be submitted through a screening committee that would, as is the case with UNAT appeals, be granted authority from the General Assembly to request opinions.[86]

Allowing domestic courts to obtain advisory opinions has a number of potential benefits. It would (a) assist in the rendering of justice, (b) promote uniformity in the interpretation of international law, (c) strengthen the ICJ's constituency by establishing links to domestic judicial systems, (d) provide indirect access to the Court by individuals and corporations, and (e) expand the work of the Court.

84/ *See* S.Schwebel, *Preliminary Rulings by the International Court of Justice at the Instance of National Courts*, 28 Va. J. Int'l L. 495 (1988).

85/ Some have argued, however, that the European Court is not an appropriate model because it is in essence a supra-national court, not an international court, and it must be viewed as part of the judicial system of member states. *See* S. Rosenne, *Preliminary Rulings by the International Court of Justice and the Instance of National Courts: A Reply*, 29 Va. J. Int'l L. 401, 405 (1989).

The Law of the Sea Convention contains a similar provision. Article 177 provides that under some circumstances an arbitral tribunal must obtain a ruling from the Sea Bed Disputes Chamber, and must issue its award in conformity with the ruling so obtained. The American Convention on Human Rights provides that member states may consult with the Inter-American Court of Human Rights regarding the interpretation of human rights treaties and states may request opinions concerning the compatibility of their domestic laws with such treaties.

86/ It is not absolutely clear that domestic courts will be able to obtain advisory opinions without a Statute amendment. The concept of advisory opinions at the request of states was expressly rejected at the San Francisco Conference when it was drafting the Statute, and a number of judges have expressed dissatisfaction with the way advisory opinions are requested in administrative tribunal cases. Some commentators believe that the Court might be unwilling to expand further this method of obtaining advisory opinions to new circumstances. Nonetheless, an attempt should be made to set up a system by which domestic courts can obtain the advice of the ICJ.

> That the Court has fallen into a relative disuse is a reflection of the attitude of states. Until states that have access to the World Court are more willing to use it . . . widening access to the Court for lesser entities will be of secondary importance. . . . Moreover, states unwilling to entrust their disputes with other states to the Court will be even more unwilling to agree to their nationals appearing before the Court in a dispute with their state . . . .
>
> *1976 State Department Report*

On the other hand, the problem of uniformity in the application of international law by domestic courts may be exaggerated, and the degree to which national courts would utilize such a power is open to question. Many domestic courts would justifiably be concerned about the delay inherent in such a procedure. Others are jealous of their power and would be unwilling to refer matters to the ICJ which they feel competent to decide themselves. The executive authority of some states might be reluctant to allow its courts to seek advisory opinions on sensitive matters. Where the necessary jurisdictional nexus does not exist for a state to initiate a contentious proceeding against another state, it might utilize this procedure to obtain an advisory opinion on the matter in dispute. Many states might oppose setting up a mechanism by which another state could request an advisory opinion on matters in which they may be vitally interested.[87]

Even if the Statute can be amended to provide for advisory opinions upon state requests, it might be advisable to keep a committee in the process to screen out requests that are frivolous or harassing. The screening committee used in administrative tribunal cases is political in makeup. Any screening committee established by the General Assembly to review requests from national courts should, if possible, be kept non-political. Perhaps, the members could be selected by the International Law Commission. As noted above, a committee should screen out only requests that are clearly inappropriate, not impose its judgement on the merits of the request. Accordingly any committee, whether screening requests for advisory opinions from states, organizations or individuals, should be permitted to request an opinions with less than majority vote (e.g., 30 to 40 percent).

Nothing in this proposal would require domestic courts to request advisory opinions or would make any advice received binding upon them. Nonetheless, once a system is established for obtaining advisory opinions, states could include provisions in treaties requiring requests for advisory opinions under specified circumstances and making such opinions binding.[88]

87/ Some proposals also advocate allowing the executive branch of a state to request advisory opinions. The potential for abuse would be greater under such circumstances, but use of a screening committee could reduce this potential.

88/ It is possible that any provision making ICJ determinations binding on U.S. courts could run afoul of Article III of the U.S. Constitution that vests the judicial power of the U.S. in the federal court system. However, it can also be argued that what is being exercised in such cases is not the "judicial power of the U.S.," but rather the judicial power of the world community. In any event, allowing U.S. courts to obtain non-binding opinions from the ICJ should not raise any problems.

4. Opening the Court to Individuals & Corporations

Under the current system, the ICJ can hear cases involving a claim by an individual (or corporation) against a foreign state only if the individual's state espouses the claim on his behalf. Whether a state asserts a claim on behalf of one of its citizens may depend more on the relations between the states concerned than upon the merits of the claim. States are reasonably reluctant to espouse claims where they might aggravate tensions with another state. If a mechanism is established whereby domestic courts can obtain advisory opinions from the ICJ, and this mechanism is actually used, it will give individuals, corporations, and other such entities indirect access to the Court. By allowing individuals some access to the ICJ (even if indirect) the need for states to espouse claims on behalf of their nationals should be reduced.

Proposals to expand the circumstances under which individuals can directly petition a screening committee for referral of a case for an advisory opinion are probably not feasible at this time. While it might be possible to get enough nations to accept the idea that an individual should be permitted to obtain an opinion on a dispute with a foreign state, any scheme that would allow an individual to obtain an advisory opinion concerning a dispute with his own state (such as over human rights violations) would likely be resisted by many states.

A change in the Court's rules with respect to advisory opinions involving individuals is needed. Under the ICJ's current practice, individuals involved in appeals from administrative tribunals are not permitted to appear directly before the Court. This limitation is based upon the fact that the Statute only provides for receipt of statements from states and international organizations. The individual's statement, is however, forwarded to the Court through the organizations.[89] Oral argument is often dispensed with because the Statute and Rules do not provide for participation of individuals in oral argument and the Court does not wish to appear unfair by allowing the organization and interested states to present argument while denying the same opportunity to the individual. The drawback to this is that oral argument might be useful in clarifying the position of the parties. The Court's construction of the Statute is unduly restrictive. While the Statute does not specifically provide for appearances by individuals, neither does it prohibit them. Interpreting the Statute to permit the ICJ to receive submissions and argument from anyone who might be able to shed light on the question at hand would not be unreasonable.[90] The Court should modify its rules to provide for the fullest participation possible of the actual parties in interest.

89/ Article 65(2) of the Statute requires that all documents likely to shed light on the issue be included with the request. In accordance with this provision, the UNAT statute requires the Secretary General to transmit the views of the individual to the Court together with the request for an opinion.

90/ This is no less reasonable a construction of the Statute than, as discussed below, is the Court's construction of the provisions relating to special chambers. The Statute provides for consultation with the parties concerning the number of judges that will make up the chamber. However, the Court also consults with them and follows their wishes as to the identity of the judges as well. Alternatively, the Court could appoint a commission of enquiry to obtain evidence and argument from the individual and other interested parties.

VI. Admissibility

In addition to contesting jurisdiction, respondent states may argue that the dispute is not suitable for judicial resolution. The admissibility of a case is a preliminary matter that is usually decided simultaneously with jurisdiction. Nonetheless, as with questions of jurisdiction, the Court may defer ruling on admissibility until the merits phase.

Objections raised by respondents to the competence of the Court have included the lack of standing of the applicant to assert the claim, the absence of an essential party,[91] the case becoming moot, the failure to exhaust domestic or diplomatic remedies, the inability of the Court to resolve the entire dispute between the parties, and the contention that the matter should be decided by the Security Council. Several cases have dealt with the standing of the applicant state to bring the complaint. For example, although only states can be parties before the Court, states may espouse claims on behalf of individuals or corporations. International law, however, limits this right to espouse a private claim to instances where the state has a close relationship to the aggrieved party. *Barcelona Traction* involved the seizure by Spain through a bankruptcy proceeding of the assets of a Canadian corporation. Belgium instituted the proceeding against Spain to recover damages on behalf of its nationals, who owned most of the shares of the corporation. The Court found the case inadmissible, holding that the fact that the shareholders were Belgian was insufficient to give Belgium standing to espouse the claim of a Canadian corporation.[92]

The *South West Africa Cases* also raised the issue of standing. South Africa administered South West Africa (now Namibia) under a Mandate issued by the League of Nations. Ethiopia and Liberia brought this action as former members of the League, charging that South Africa had violated its obligations under the mandate. By the narrowest of margins (8 to 7) the Court found that while South Africa remained bound by the terms of the mandate, the right to enforce the mandate had not devolved upon the individual states that were members of the former

---

91/ The *Monetary Gold* case was found to be inadmissible because of the absence of Albania, the principal party whose interest was at stake. But in *Nicaragua*, the ICJ rejected the contention that the case should be dismissed because of the absence of other Central American states involved in the conflict. For a detailed discussion of the problems involved with multiparty disputes see Part IX(B), *infra.*

92/ *Nottebohm (Lict. v. Guat.)*, 1955 I.C.J. 4, concerned a German citizen who had long lived in Guatemala. In 1939, Nottebohm obtained Liechtensteinian citizenship, primarily to avoid difficulties associated with having German nationality during the war. Nonetheless, following his return to Guatemala he was interned until the end of the war and his property confiscated. Liechtenstein initiated this case against Guatemala to recover compensation on Nottebohm's behalf. The ICJ determined that while states may grant citizenship to whomever they want, such citizenship did not necessarily confer upon the state a right to espouse claims on behalf of the individual where there is no real bond between the individual and the state. The Court noted that at the time of his naturalization Nottebohm had never resided in Liechtenstein, did not intend to reside in Liechtenstein, had no family ties there, and did not participate in its public life. Under these circumstances, the Court concluded that Guatemala was not required to recognize Nottebohm's naturalization and that the case was inadmissible because Liechtenstein could not espouse his claim.

League. The U.N., as the League's successor, however, did have limited rights to enforce the mandate. Consequently, Ethiopia and Liberia did not have standing to bring the case.[93]

In *Northern Cameroons*, Cameroon complained of the manner in which the U.K. administered its Trusteeship over the northern Cameroons and the plebiscite it conducted that resulted in the Northern Cameroons being joined to Nigeria. The ICJ concluded that the case was inadmissible because even if it found in favor of Cameroon, the judgment would be meaningless since the rights and obligations of the U.K. with respect to the Northern Cameroons had been terminated. The Court found the *Nuclear Test Cases*, in which Australia and New Zealand complained of French atmospheric nuclear testing in Polynesia, to be moot when France publicly declared that it would cease such tests.

Failure of the aggrieved state to exhaust its remedies under domestic law was the basis for dismissal of the *Interhandel Case*. On the other hand, it is not necessary to exhaust possibilities of diplomatic negotiations before resorting to the court.[94] In *Nicaragua* the Court rejected the argument advanced by the U.S. that the case was inadmissible because the Contadora process was continuing.[95] The fact that only one aspect of a complex dispute between nations is before the ICJ does not necessarily make a case inadmissible. In the *Hostages* case, Iran contended that the holding of U.S. diplomats hostage was secondary and marginal to an overall situation involving 25 years of U.S. interference in Iranian affairs, and that it could not be examined separately from the underlying political dispute between it and the U.S. The Court rejected this argument, stating:

> [L]egal disputes between sovereign States by their very nature are likely to occur in political contexts, and often form only one element in a wider . . . political dispute . . . . Yet never has the view been put forward that, because a legal dispute submitted to the Court is only one aspect of a political dispute, the Court should decline to resolve for the parties the legal question at issue between them. If the Court were, contrary to its settled jurisprudence, to adopt such a view, it would impose a far-reaching and unwarranted restriction upon the role of the Court in the peaceful solution of international disputes.[96]

Of course, the inviolability of diplomats and diplomatic missions is fundamental to international law, and the principal is well established that irrespective of the animosity between states,

---

93/ South Africa's administration of South West Africa also generated four advisory opinions: *International Status of South West Africa*, 1950 I.C.J. 128; *Voting Procedures on Questions Relating to Reports & Petitions Concerning the Territory of South West Africa*, 1955 I.C.J. 67; *Admissibility of Hearings of Petitioners by the Committee on South West Africa*, 1956 I.C.J. 23; *Legal Consequences for States of the Continued Presence of South Africa in Namibia Notwithstanding Security Council Resolution 276 (1970)*, 1971 I.C.J. 16.

94/ Of course, if the basis for jurisdiction (a compromissory clause or declaration under the optional clause) specifically requires exhaustion of diplomatic means of settlement, the Court should honor that requirement. However, the Court will not insist on further negotiations where they are unlikely to be productive. In this regard, the Court in *Nicaragua* rejected the U.S. position that jurisdiction under the FCN treaty should be denied because the possibilities of negotiation had not been exhausted.

95/ The ICJ also noted that even if the Contadora process were viewed as a regional arrangement, Article 52(2) of the Charter which requires parties to seek regional resolution of disputes before submitting them to the Security Council does not apply to submission of cases to the Court. *See also Right of Passage Over Indian Territory (Port. v. India)*, 1957 I.C.J. 125 (Preliminary Objections); *Aegean Sea Continental Shelf (Greece v. Turkey)*, 1978 I.C.J. 3 (Jurisdiction).

96/ 1980 I.C.J. 3, 20.

diplomats and embassies must be respected. It was therefore clear that the issue of taking diplomats hostage could be divorced from the underlying dispute between Iran and the U.S. In another situation, however, the ICJ might reasonably find that the dispute, as submitted to the Court, is so intertwined with other issues that it must be considered only in its larger context.

> I want to see the judicial organ and the political organs of the United Nations both working in harness much more than hitherto. . . . [T]he aim I have in view is that the Court and the law it applies should be seen much more readily and commonly to be relevant to most disputed situations, if only to a legal component of those situations, and that it should be much more readily seen that the Court itself could be used for its proper legal purpose by the Security Council and the General Assembly, and by other bodies entitled to employ the Court's advisory jurisdiction, in matters that are not essentially legal in the overall view, but perhaps highly political.
>
> *ICJ President Sir Robert Jennings*
> *Address to the General Assembly (1991)*

Among the most controversial aspects of *Nicaragua* concerned the proper role of the Court in disputes involving ongoing hostilities. The U.S. contended that whether its actions constituted an unlawful use of armed force or whether they were a reasonable exercise of its inherent right to collective self-defense were questions that are committed under the U.N. Charter to the Security Council. The U.S. noted that Article 24 of the Charter confers upon the Security Council "primary responsibility for the maintenance of international peace and security," and Article 39 provides that the Security Council "shall determine" the existence of any threat to peace. The U.S. concluded that the drafters of the Charter envisioned that disputes of this nature would be decided by the Council, not by the Court. It further noted that Nicaragua had made the same claims to the Security Council and that the ICJ proceeding was in fact an appeal from the Security Council's action (or in this case inaction)—an appellate power that the Court does not possess. The U.S. also observed that under Article 51, nations retain their right to individual or collective self-defense "until the Security Council has taken measures necessary to maintain international peace and security." The U.S. maintained that nations have full discretion to decide whether self-defense is warranted until the Security Council acts on the matter. Thus, according to the U.S., the ICJ has no power to review its exercise of collective self-defense.

The ICJ unanimously rejected these contentions. The Court, quite reasonably, concluded that judicial resolution of the dispute was not incompatible with the role of the Security Council. The ICJ observed that under the Charter, the Security Council's responsibility for maintaining peace is *primary,* not *exclusive*. And, under Article 12, the General Assembly is specifically barred from making recommendations with respect to disputes under consideration by the Security Council, but there is no similar prohibition on the Court. The Court rejected the contention that the reasonableness of actions allegedly taken in self-defense is, until the Security Council considers the matter, solely within the discretion of the nation taking them. Self-defense is a legal "right." Article 51's provision that nothing in the Charter is intended to impair that right until the Security Council acts does not imply that the scope of that right is unfettered and incapable of legal determination. The Court concluded that there is nothing in the Charter that barred the consideration of Nicaragua's claims.[97]

Nor does Court review of matters considered by the Security Council constitute an "appeal." The Court and the Council play very different roles. The role of the ICJ is to adjudicate disputes between nations based upon legal principles. The Council's role is to take measures to insure peace, even if those measures are not strictly compatible with legal rights. For example, a state may unlawfully invade another state. The Security Council may order a cease fire to restore peace even if that results in the aggressor state retaining control over some territory of the innocent state. As judge Schwebel explained:

> [W]hile the Security Council is invested by the Charter with the authority to determine the existence of an act of aggression, it does not act as a court in making such determination. It may arrive at a determination of aggression . . . for political reasons. However compelling the facts which could give rise to a determination of aggression, the Security Council acts within its rights when it decides that to make such a determination will set back the cause of peace rather than advance it. In short, the Security Council is a political organ which acts for political reasons. It may take legal considerations into account but, unlike a court, is not bound to apply them.[98]

Thus, while a determination by the Security Council might be inconsistent with the legal rights of the parties as determined by the ICJ, this does not make the Council's determination either improper or illegal, or bar the ICJ from determining those legal rights. Where jurisdiction is present, either party has the right to have the Court determine their legal rights, which may of course influence the Council and world opinion. At the same time, states are also obligated to implement the Council's decisions under Chapter VII, even if they are otherwise inconsistent with their strict legal rights.

It is important to recognize, however, that there are practical limits to the ability of the ICJ to resolve disputes involving ongoing armed conflicts. States that have resorted to war are not likely to heed the judgment of the Court, and obtaining evidence may be particularly difficult in cases of armed conflict.

97/ While the Court's conclusions were reasonable, it relied in several respects on cases that are inapposite. It cited *Corfu Channel* and the *Aerial Incident* cases, even though they were isolated incidents and did not involve an ongoing conflict, and it relied upon the *Hostages* case, which did not involve armed hostilities.

98/ 1986 I.C.J. 14, 290 (Merits) (Schwebel, J).

VII. Chambers

The Court's Statute allows the parties to elect to have cases heard by chambers, i.e., by panels containing fewer than all of the judges. Both the ICJ and PCIJ Statutes created a chamber of summary procedure. The ICJ chamber is composed of five judges, the PCIJ had three. In addition, both Statutes provide for chambers to deal with specified categories of disputes. The PCIJ Statute created two chambers, one to deal with labor cases and the other with transit and communications cases. The ICJ Statute abandoned the detailed provision of the PCIJ Statute for these two chambers. Instead Article 26(1) gives the Court a general power to form "one or more Chambers, composed of three or more judges as the Court might determine, for dealing with particular categories of cases . . . ." Although both the PCIJ and the ICJ have dutifully elected judges to the chamber for summary procedure, it has heard only one dispute in its existence—a dispute in 1924 between Greece and Bulgaria.[99] The PCIJ chambers for labor cases and transit and communications cases were never called upon. The ICJ first exercised its authority to create a chamber for a particular category of cases in 1993 when it created a chamber of seven judges to hear environmental disputes. That chamber has not yet been called upon to hear a case.

A. Ad Hoc Chambers

The ICJ Statute contained an innovation that was not present in the PCIJ Statute. Article 26(2) reads, "The Court may at any time form a chamber for dealing with a particular case. The number of judges to constitute such a chamber shall be determined by the Court with the approval of the parties." In 1979, the U.S. and Canada became the first parties to request that a case be heard by such an *ad hoc* chamber, when they submitted the *Gulf of Maine* case pursuant to a special agreement. Since then, three other cases have been heard by ad hoc chambers: In 1987 the Court created a chamber to hear *Frontier Dispute (Burkina Faso v. Mali)*, and in 1987 it created chambers to hear *ELSI* and *Land, Island & Maritime Frontier Dispute (El. Sal. v. Hond.).*

The use of *ad hoc* chambers was encouraged by the 1978 amendments to the Court's Rules. Article 17 of the Rules provides that (1) a request for formation of a chamber may be filed at any time up to the closure of the written proceedings, (2) the President shall ascertain the parties' views regarding the composition of the chamber, (3) the Court shall proceed to elect the chamber after it has determined, with the approval of the parties, the number of judges who shall constitute the chamber, and (4) members of the chamber whose terms of office on the Court have expired shall continue to sit in all phases of the case being heard by the chamber. These revised rules contained two significant changes. The requirement that the President consult with the parties to ascertain their views regarding not only the number of judges, but also the composition of the chamber, allows the parties significant control over

---

99/ There were actually two linked cases regarding this dispute: *Treaty of Neuilly, Art. 179, Annex ¶ 4 (Interpretation)*, 1924 P.C.I.J. (ser. A) No. 3 (Judgment of Sept. 12); *Interpretation of Judgment No. 3*, 1925 P.C.I.J. (ser. A) (Judgment of March 26).

the makeup of the chamber. The provision allowing a judge whose term of office has expired to continue to serve on the chamber until conclusion of the case helps ensure that makeup of the chamber is unlikely to change. This is in contrast to cases heard by the full Court, where judges continue to serve only if oral argument has been held and then only to the conclusion of that particular phase of the case.[100]

As a practical matter, these provisions allow the parties to specify the composition of the chamber. This was abundantly clear in the special agreement which accompanied the *compromis* by which the U.S. and Canada submitted the *Gulf of Maine* case. It provided that the case would be withdrawn and referred to arbitration if the chamber was not constituted as specified by the parties, and that if a vacancy should occur in the chamber the parties would agree to withdraw the case if the vacancy was not filled by a mutually acceptable judge. The Court, in the order establishing the chamber, indicated that it elected the judges specified by the parties.

To date, all requests for chambers have been part of special agreements (even though jurisdiction in the *ELSI* case was based upon a compromissory clause). Provisions for chambers proceedings could, however, be included in the compromissory clauses of treaties. To be effective, such a compromissory clause must contain a method for agreeing upon the judges if the parties can not agree. Otherwise, the clause would be meaningless since either party could obstruct the litigation by simply refusing to agree to a fair composition of the chamber. One method would be to allow each party to exclude between three and five judges from consideration for the chamber and allowing the parties to withdraw the case if any of these judges are elected to the chamber.[101]

Ad hoc chambers combine many of the attractive elements of arbitration with the benefits and prestige of an established court. They satisfy the desire of parties to have their disputes settled by a tribunal of their own choosing. Parties can select judges with expertise in the subject of the dispute while eliminating those whom they think may be biased. *Ad hoc* chambers are, however, more than mere arbitral tribunals composed of Court judges.[102] A

100/ Both of these provisions are within the scope of the Statute, which provides that judges "shall finish any case which they may have begun." Art. 13(3). They merely involve different interpretations of the word "begun."

101/ A reservation to a declaration under the optional clause requiring a chamber is more problematic. To be meaningful, such a reservation would have to contain some method for agreeing upon which judges would be acceptable. Some commentators have questioned whether such a reservation would be valid under the Statute because it seeks to impose obligations on the other party after the Court has been seized, and because it would give a party a unilateral right to withdraw if the requested composition is not accepted by the Court. The issue is whether this can be done through a reservation under the optional clause. *See* Leigh & Ramsey, *supra* note 44, at 117—22.

102/ Arbitral tribunals composed of ICJ judges have been used in the past. In the *Beagle Channel Arbitration* between Chile and Argentina in the 1970's, Chile preferred arbitration by the British Government, while Argentina, in view of its dispute with the U.K. over the Falkland (Malvinas) Islands, preferred recourse to the ICJ. They settled on arbitration before a panel of five ICJ judges, none of whom were nationals of the disputants. *The Beagle Channel Arbitration*, 71 AM. J. INT'L L. 733 (1977). Argentina rejected the arbitration award, and Papal mediation ensued. The final settlement did not differ significantly from the arbitral award. 24 I.L.M. 1 (1978).

The use of ICJ judges as arbitrators reached an extreme in the arbitration in the early 1980's of a maritime boundary dispute between Guinea and Guinea Bissau. The parties selected three ICJ judges as

(Cont'd)

chamber of the Court may be more predictable in its procedures and how it applies the law than would an arbitral tribunal. In arbitration, the parties have more flexibility in selecting procedures to be used, while a chamber would follow the Court's Rules. An arbitration award is not equivalent to a judgment by the Court, which may in theory be enforced by the Security Council. Moreover, the Court has higher visibility and prestige than would an arbitral panel; consequently, its decision may be more likely to settle the matter. Finally, as a practical matter, a chamber may be less expensive than arbitration, since the costs of the Court are borne by the U.N., while those of arbitral panels are borne by the parties.

Chamber proceedings differ from proceedings before the full court in several significant ways. As a practical matter, it may be easier for the parties to arrange for use of a language other than English or French and to arrange for the proceedings to be conducted at a location more convenient to them than The Hague. In addition, the Rules pertaining to all chambers provide for a slightly simplified procedure, including only one submission by each party. However, this and most other provisions in the rules can be modified upon agreement between the parties and the Court, and the chamber proceedings conducted so far have not been noticeably speedier than proceedings before the full Court. Finally, judges that are nationals of the parties, especially *ad hoc* judges, would have greater influence in a smaller chamber. There is also a greater chance that chambers will issue judgments that are based upon compromise rather than strict application of the law, but this would not necessarily be undesirable.

Ad hoc chamber proceedings have not been without controversy. Some judges and commentators maintain that allowing the parties to dictate to the Court who should make up a chamber is inconsistent with the Statute,[103] deprives the Court of its freedom of choice, and leads to chambers that are ideologically and geographically unbalanced.[104] Certainly, the Statute's requirement that the Court as a whole represent all the major forms of civilization and legal systems in the world was not intended to apply to individual chambers. Indeed, it would be impossible to maintain such a requirement for a chamber of only five judges (especially if two were *ad hoc* judges). Moreover, even if a particular chamber is in someone's opinion "unbalanced," this does not mean that it cannot render a reasoned and fair judgment. There is also no merit to the charge that allowing the parties to request, or even require, that

---

102/ (Cont'd)
arbitrators, agreed to use the Rules of the Court, held the proceedings at The Hague, and selected the deputy registrar of the Court as the registrar of the Tribunal. A. Zimmerman, *Ad Hoc Chambers of the International Court of Justice*, 8 DIK. J. INT'L L. 1, 6—7 (1989). Since the ICJ's Rules had been amended to facilitate the use of *ad hoc* chambers by the time this arbitration was conducted, it is a mystery why the parties did not utilize that provision. Perhaps, they were unsure of how chamber proceedings would work out as the first chamber proceeding, the *Gulf of Maine* case, had not yet been concluded.

103/ *See Land, Island & Maritime Frontier Dispute (El Sal. v. Hond.)*, 1990 I.C.J. 3, 18 (Intervention) (Shahabuddeen, J., Dissenting). Because the Statute provides only that the parties shall agree to the number of judges, the argument is that consultation concerning the identity of the judges is inconsistent with the Statute. This argument is without merit. Silence on the issue does not mean it cannot be done. The Statute places no limit on the factors that the Court can consider in electing a chamber.

104/ Complaints were made that the *Gulf of Maine* chamber was composed exclusively of judges from North America and Western Europe. This criticism is unwarranted. The judgment shows no evidence of a pro-Western bias. Moreover, the original agreement between the U.S. and Canada called for a chamber that was more geographically balanced, but it had to be modified upon the deaths of three of the judges.

particular judges be on a chamber infringes upon the rights of the Court to elect the judges. As Judge Oda noted:

> The Court, being sovereign in judicial proceedings, is free to choose any composition it likes; yet the possibility must also be borne in mind that sovereign States have the legal right to withdraw a case if they prefer a composition different from that determined by the Court. In practical terms, therefore, it is inevitable, if a chamber is to be viable, that its composition must result from a consensus between the Parties and the Court. To ensure that viability, it accordingly behooves the Court to take account of the views of the Parties when proceeding to the election. Nevertheless, the chamber is a component of the Court . . . and the process of election . . . should be as judicially impartial as its subsequent functioning.[105]

Thus, while the Court should generally accede to the requests of the parties, on rare occasions it may wish to disregard them and elect other judges. This should be done if the Court believes that a chamber constituted as the parties request would be unfair to any state or if it would endanger the credibility of the Court.

The primary purpose of the ICJ is to decide cases at hand. However, incidental to this purpose, the ICJ aids the development of international law by providing guides to how the law will be applied in future cases. The Statute provides that a judgment by a chamber shall have the same force and effect as one rendered by the full Court. Thus, a chamber decision will be equally effective in deciding the case, and is as enforceable as a decision by the full Court. But, a chamber judgment may not necessarily provide as clear a guide to how the law will be applied in future cases. Under the Statute, a decision is binding only on the parties and with respect to the instant dispute; the legal principles expressed in a decision are not binding upon the Court in future cases. As a practical matter though, the Court has followed its precedents when deciding subsequent cases. It remains to be seen whether the Court will give as much deference to chamber decisions. The precedential value of a chamber judgment should, as with a judgment by the full Court, be based upon the quality of its reasoning. To the extent that the ICJ believes that a decision resulted from, e.g., compromise or a chamber whose makeup was unbalanced, the Court should be free, as it is with respect to a decision by the full Court, to discount the decision.[106] While resort to chambers may increase the chance of inconsistent decisions being rendered by different chambers, it may also increase the number of disputes that are peacefully resolved by the Court. While inconsistent or unreasoned decisions by chambers should be rare, too many could undermine the authority of ICJ judgments and lead to doubts about whether a particular chamber decision accurately reflects international law.

105/ *Land, Island & Maritime Frontier Dispute (El. Sal. v. Hond.)*, 1987 I.C.J. at 13 (Oda, J, declaration).

106/ The judgment in *Gulf of Maine* figured in the subsequent *Continental Shelf (Libya v. Malta)*, 1985 I.C.J. 13, and the fact that it was issued by a chamber did not cause it to be discounted by the Court.

B. Chambers Procedures Need Clarification

There are a number of questions pertaining to chambers that are not adequately answered by the Rules or by the limited experience with them to date. A central issue is the division of responsibilities for a case between the chamber and the full Court. Should preliminary matters, such as jurisdiction and requests for interim measures of protection, be heard by the chamber or the full Court? As a general rule, it seems that the chamber should hear all matters concerning a case if it has been constituted at the time the issue arises. If there is no urgency a pending request to form a chamber should take precedence over preliminary rulings.[107] However, requests for interim measures are frequently urgent and the full Court should rule on them if waiting until election of the chamber would cause unwarranted delay. Jurisdictional issues should usually be decided by the chamber. However, if the question of whether the parties have consented to use of a chamber is bound up with the question of jurisdiction, jurisdiction may have to be decided by the full Court. For example, jurisdiction might be claimed based upon a compromissory clause that also provides for adjudication by a chamber. If the respondent contests the allegation that the compromissory clause is applicable to the dispute, it cannot be said to have agreed to the use of a chamber until the Court determines that the compromissory clause is applicable.[108]

Requests for intervention by third states present especially difficult issues. The Court should be especially sensitive about doing anything that would prejudice third parties. It would seem that because the intervention is merely incidental to the main proceeding, the intervenor should not be able to block the request that the case be heard by a chamber. The more important issue is whether an intervenor should be consulted regarding the composition of the chamber. In 1990, Nicaragua sought to intervene in a maritime boundary dispute between El Salvador and Honduras. Although a chamber had been constituted more than two years earlier, Nicaragua asked that its request be considered by the full Court. Nicaragua alleged that it would be prejudiced if the case were heard by a chamber formulated in accordance with the wishes of El Salvador and Honduras. Nicaragua stated that if its request to intervene were granted, it would ask that the chamber be reconstituted. The ICJ found that Nicaragua's intervention request must be heard by the chamber.[109] It found in essence that Nicaragua must accept the procedural status of the case at the time it filed its intervention request. This is certainly reasonable, especially in view of Nicaragua's more than two year delay in seeking to intervene.

107/ The Court has not been entirely consistent in its treatment of these matters. For example, in three of the cases the full Court fixed the time limits for filing of pleadings under Article 92(1) of the Rules, but the chamber fixed these limits in the *Land, Island & Maritime Frontier Dispute*. Zimmermann, *supra* note 102, at 22. It would be preferable for such decisions to be made by the chambers.

108/ The Court's Rules need to be clarified in a number of areas pertaining to the operation of chambers. For example, the Rules provide that where a judgment was heard by a chamber, requests for interpretation or revision of the judgment shall be determined by that chamber. Clearly, the Chamber for Summary Procedure and special chambers dealing with specific issues are continuing bodies so that a request for interpretation or revision would be heard by that chamber even if its composition has changed. However, *ad hoc* chambers cease to exist after the conclusion of the case. The members of the chamber may not even be on the Court when the request is filed. Even if they remain on the Court it is not clear whether they would hear a request for revision or interpretation.

109/ *Land, Island & Maritime Frontier Dispute (El Sal. v. Hond.)*, 1990 I.C.J. 3. (Intervention).

The case did not resolve the more difficult question of whether a state that requests intervention before a chamber is elected should be consulted about the makeup of the chamber. Such consultation would be wise, and if the Court finds that the composition of the chamber as requested by the parties might be prejudicial to the intervenor, the Court should hesitate to accept that composition. Indeed, even if there is no pending intervention request, the Court may wish to avoid creating any chamber that might appear to be prejudicial to any third party.

VIII. MAKING PROVISIONAL MEASURES MORE EFFECTIVE

Article 41 of the Statute gives the Court authority to indicate provisional measures.[110] Litigation before the ICJ can be lengthy. Several years can elapse between the filing of a case and the Court's final judgment, and actions by a party during the pendency of a case could do irreparable injury to the other party that would render any judgment of the Court meaningless. The purpose of provisional measures is to protect the interests of both parties until the final decision is reached on the merits. By providing interim judicial relief, the Court may also forestall a party from engaging in self-help and thereby endangering world peace. For example, in *Fisheries Jurisdiction*, where the U.K. and Germany contested Iceland's assertion of fisheries jurisdiction to 50 miles, the ICJ restrained enforcement of Icelandic regulations beyond 12 miles and imposed catch limits of British and German ships fishing within 50 miles. In the *Hostages* case, the provisional measures if complied with would have given the U.S. most of what it sought on the merits, i.e. return of the embassy premises to the U.S. and release of the hostages. Provisional measures are not appropriate in all cases. Many proceedings do not involve a risk of irreparable injury and in others the parties may agree to voluntarily restrain their actions.[111]

Promptness in indicating provisional measures may be crucial. Delay could make them meaningless by allowing irreparably injury. Accordingly, the Court's rules provide that any party may request provisional measures at any time during the course of a proceeding and that such requests shall have priority over other matters. Measures are imposed only after a hearing. Pending convening of the Court, the rules authorize the President to "call upon the parties to act in such a way as will enable any order the Court may make on the request for provisional measures to have its appropriate effects."[112] In recent years, it has taken the Court about one month to rule on requests for provisional measures.

The time restraints inherent in requests for provisional measures necessarily prevent the ICJ from considering fully jurisdiction, admissibility or the merits of the case, and a ruling on provisional measures is not intended to prejudge these issues. The question of jurisdiction has been especially problematic. How can the Court impose provisional measures upon a state

---

110/ For a discussion of provisional measures generally, see B. Oxman *Jurisdiction & the Power to Indicate Provisional Measures*, in CROSSROADS, *supra* note 23, at 323.

111/ The nature of provisional measures, i.e., whether they are a legally binding judgment or are merely recommendatory has been subject to some dispute. The better view is that they are binding. *See* M. O'Connell, *The Prospects for Enforcing Monetary Judgments of the International Court of Justice*, 30 Va J. Int'l L. 891, 900—01 (1990). Moreover, a provision in another treaty or convention may specify that they are binding. *See* General Act, *supra* note 53, at Art. 33(1). It is also unclear whether an order indicating provisional measures can, like a final judgment, be enforced by the Security Council.

112/ Rules, Art. 74(4). Earlier versions of the Rules gave the President greater powers in this regard. The 1922 PCIJ Rules provided that the President could indicate provisional measures when the Court was not sitting. Rules in effect for the PCIJ after 1936 and for the ICJ until 1978 provided that pending a meeting of the Court, the President shall "take such measures as appear to him necessary in order to enable the Court to give an effective decision." *See* Oxman, *supra* note 110, at 324 n.8.

where it might not have jurisdiction over the case? In many circumstances, if the Court were to take the time to definitively resolve the matter of jurisdiction it would defeat the purpose of provisional measures. On the other hand, there is a patent unfairness in imposing measures where there is no jurisdiction. While there are differences of opinion among the judges as to the standards to be applied, the Court tends to take a position somewhere between holding that jurisdiction is irrelevant to provisional measures and holding that jurisdiction must be proved conclusively.[113] The members of the Court have not agreed, however, on a clear and consistent test to resolve this jurisdictional dilemma. In *Nicaragua*, the Court explained that:

> [O]n a request for provisional measures the Court need not . . . finally satisfy itself that it has jurisdiction on the merits of the case, or, as the case may be, that an objection taken to jurisdiction is well-founded, yet it ought not to indicate such measures unless the provisions invoked by the Applicant appear, prima facie, to afford a basis on which the jurisdiction of the Court might be founded.[114]

Commentators, as well as members of the Court, usually overemphasize the importance of jurisdiction to the ability of the ICJ to grant interim relief. A distinction must be made between jurisdiction to decide the merits of the case and the power of the Court to order provisional measures. The ICJ's authority over the merits is limited by Article 36 to instances where states have conferred jurisdiction on the Court, but its authority to direct interim relief comes from Article 41 which applies to all states that are parties to the Statute.[115]

In deciding provisional measures, the Court emphasizes jurisdiction to the near exclusion of other factors related to whether the party requesting interim relief is likely to succeed on the merits. Whenever provisional measures are imposed and the party requesting them does not ultimately prevail, the other party will have been restrained from performing actions that, in retrospect, it had every right to perform. The potential injury from such restraint does not depend upon whether the reason the applicant failed to succeed was lack of jurisdiction, inadmissibility, or the state of the applicable law. The Court's rulings on provisional measures contain little discussion of the probability that the applicant will ultimately prevail. Another

---

113/ A few judges have taken the extreme position that jurisdiction must be certain. For example, in his separate opinion in *Aegean Sea (Greece v. Turk.)*, 1976 I.C.J. 3, 22, Judge Morozov stated that "the Court has no right to consider . . . the question of interim measures of protection, before it has satisfied itself that it has jurisdiction . . . ." For most judges, however, the critical issue is whether there is sufficient probability that jurisdiction exists.

114/ 1984 I.C.J. at 442 (jurisdiction and admissibility Judgment of Nov. 26). Article 290 of the Convention on the Law of the Sea also allows for provisional measures, not only to protect the rights of the parties, but also to "prevent serious harm to the marine environment." The jurisdictional nexus is somewhat tighter than for the ICJ, in that the tribunal to which the case is submitted must "consider that *prima facie* it *has* jurisdiction." (emphasis added.)

115/ The ICJ explained this distinction in dismissing *Anglo-Iranian Oil Co.*, 1952 I.C.J. 93, 102-03 (Jurisdiction Judgment of July 22), after it had indicated provisional measures:

> While the Court derived its power to indicate these provisional measures from the special provisions contained in Article 41 of the Statute, it must now derive its jurisdiction to deal with the merits of the case from the general rules laid down in Article 36 of the Statute. These general rules, which are entirely different from the special provisions of Article 41, are based on the principle that the jurisdiction of the Court to deal with and decide a case on the merits depends on the will of the Parties.

problem is compensation where the party that was restrained ultimately prevails. The Court has never considered such compensation. The practice of U.S. courts when ruling on motions for preliminary injunctions could serve as a model for the ICJ. U.S. courts weigh a number of factors in determining whether interim relief should be granted: (1) the probability of success on the merits; (2) the degree of irreparable harm the plaintiff would suffer if relief is denied; (3) the potential harm to the defendant if relief is granted; and (4) the public interest. In addition, the party requesting interim relief is usually required to indemnify the defendant if he loses on the merits and may be required to post a bond to assure indemnification.

These criteria could be adapted to World Court practice. Questions concerning jurisdiction and admissibility would be included in the probability of success on the merits. Under this scheme a state would need to show a smaller chance of success where the potential injury was larger, but a larger probability of success where the degree of irreparable injury is small. While it would probably be inappropriate to require a state to post a bond, relief could be made contingent upon an agreement by the party requesting provisional measures to compensate the respondent if it ultimately loses the case.[116]

In considering provisional measures, the ICJ should (and does) take into account relevant Security Council resolutions. In the *Lockerbie* case, the Security Council had issued a resolution under Chapter VII on the matter. The Court found that the request for provisional measures should be denied because the resolution was binding on the parties and the measures requested by Libya would conflict with that resolution. The ICJ also denied provisional measures in *Aegean Sea*, where the Security Council had issued a non-binding resolution under Chapter VI calling on the parties to take steps to reduce tensions and to continue negotiations. The Court found that under these circumstances, provisional measures were not necessary.

As noted in the previous section, the fact that the Security Council is considering the same dispute does not make a case inadmissible. Certain decisions of the Council under Chapter VII, however, are binding on the parties and should be enforced by the Court, both at the provisional measures and merits stages of the proceeding. The ICJ was therefore correct in not doing anything in *Lockerbie* that would be inconsistent with the Security Council decision. Nonetheless, as suggested in *Lockerbie* by several dissenting judges, nothing prevents the Court from indicating provisional measures in such circumstances where they do not *conflict* with the Council resolution. Where the Security Council action is not of a binding character, the situation is less clear. While the Court in ruling on the merits of a case and the Council play very different roles, that is not true when the Court is ruling on provisional measures. The role of the ICJ at the provisional measure stage is not to rule so much on the basis of law, but to determine what must be done to stabilize the situation and protect the parties—a role very similar to that often played by the Security Council. For example, the Council under Article 40 of the Charter may suggest "provisional measures." Consequently, while the Court's determinations on provisional measures are not required to be consistent with non-binding Council actions, the Court should, as it did in *Aegean Sea*, defer as far as possible to Council resolutions when considering interim relief.

116/ Parties should be able to request that the Court reevaluate rulings on provisional measures after it has received additional evidence and argument on the merits of the case. *See* Rules, Art. 76.

IX. Improving the Handling of Multilateral Disputes

Many international disputes involve more than two states. Multilateral disputes can arise n various contexts. More than one state may file applications against a single defendant state involving the same dispute, a single state may initiate proceedings against more than one defendant, or there may be multiple states on both sides of the dispute. A third state may desire to intervene in a case because it has either an interest in the dispute itself or in how the Court will interpret the applicable law. Finally, a respondent state may contend that a complete and fair resolution of the dispute requires that a third state be a party to the case. If the third state cannot be brought before the Court, the respondent may argue that the case should be dismissed.

Neither the Statute nor the Rules of the Court deal adequately with complex multilateral disputes. The Statute clearly contemplates that there might be cases involving multiple plaintiffs or defendants since the provision relating to *ad hoc* judges provides if there are several parties with the same interest, they shall be allowed only one *ad hoc* judge among them. Nevertheless, neither the Statute nor the Court's Rules specify a means of joining parallel proceedings involving the same dispute. It may be necessary to consider questions of jurisdiction separately. However, once jurisdiction is found, joining related cases promotes efficiency and limits the chance of inconsistent decisions. Unfortunately a number of closely related cases have not been joined.[117]

A. Relaxing Limits on Intervention

The Statute does provide for third party intervention under some circumstances. Article 62 provides for intervention when a state's legal interests might be affected by a case:

> 1. Should a state consider that it has an interest of a legal nature which may be affected by the decision in the case, it may submit a request to the Court to be permitted to intervene.
>
> 2. It shall be for the Court to decide upon this request.

Article 63 deals with disputes involving multilateral conventions:

> 1. Whenever the construction of a convention to which states other than those concerned with the case are parties is in question, the Registrar shall notify all such states forthwith.
>
> 2. Every state so notified has the right to intervene in the proceedings; but if it uses this right, the construction given by the judgment will be equally binding upon it.

117/ In the *Aerial Incident* cases, Israel, the U.S. and the U.K. all initiated proceedings against Bulgaria for the downing of an Israeli civil aircraft that had inadvertently penetrated Bulgarian airspace. These cases were never consolidated, and the U.S. and the U.K. withdrew their claims after the Court found in the Israeli proceeding that Bulgaria had not accepted the Court's general jurisdiction.

There are distinct, if subtle, differences between intervention under Article 62 and under Article 63. Pursuant to Article 63 any state that is concerned with how a convention to which it is a party will be construed may intervene even if it has no direct interest in the particular dispute between the parties. Article 62, however, is limited to states that might be specifically affected by the proceeding. States meeting the criteria of Article 63 have, in theory, an absolute right to intervene, while intervention under Article 62 is left to the Court's discretion. There are differences in the scope of intervention as well. Article 63 intervention is limited to legal questions pertaining to the interpretation of the convention, and would not normally encompass factual disputes between the parties. Pursuant to Article 62, however, a state may seek to intervene with respect to any matter in dispute, including factual matters and questions of customary international law. The Rules provide that under either Article, the intervenor shall be furnished copies of the pleadings, may submit a written statement, and may participate in the oral proceedings.

The distinctions drawn in the Statute between Article 62 and Article 63 interventions are both illogical and unnecessary. There is no logical reason to favor intervention merely because the Court will construe a convention to which the intervenor is a party. States may have an equally legitimate interest in how the Court construes customary international law or interprets a treaty similar to one to which the state is a party. Moreover, it would seem that a state's right to participate should be greatest when based upon an actual interest in the dispute at hand then when based upon being a party to a convention at issue, where the intervenor might have no direct interest in the dispute.

The meaning of Article 63's provision that the construction given the convention shall be "equally binding" on intervenors is unclear. Since any judgment is binding on the parties only with respect to the case at hand, it would appear to be binding on the intervenors only with respect to the instant dispute. To the extent that a judgment has precedential effect, that effect would apply to all states irrespective of whether they participated in the proceeding. Although the Statute is silent as to whether intervenors under Article 62 are bound by the judgment, the Court indicated in *Land, Island & Maritime Frontier Dispute (El Sal. v. Hond.)*[118] that intervenors are not bound. However, there is no good reason why intervenors under either Article 62 or 63 should not both be bound.

Intervention has been sought in only a few instances. The *S.S. Wimbeledon*[119] concerned a claim brought against Germany by Britain, France, Italy, and Japan for violating the Treaty of Versailles by refusing transit through the Kiel Canal of a ship carrying arms to Poland. The PCIJ allowed Poland, which was also a party to the Treaty, to intervene. *Haya de la Torre*[120] involved Columbia's grant of asylum to Mr. Haya de la Torre in its embassy in Peru, and whether that asylum violated treaties between the two countries. Cuba, which was also a party to the treaties, sought to intervene pursuant to Article 63 in a second phase of this dispute. Its request was granted over Peru's complaint that the Cuban petition was an untimely attempt to obtain reconsideration of the earlier decision, but Cuba's participation was limited to issues that were not decided by the prior decision.

The Court denied intervention based upon Article 62 in two cases involving territorial boundaries on the continental shelf of the Mediterranean Sea. In 1981 Malta was denied

---

118/ 1990 I.C.J. 92, 135—36 (Intervention) (Chamber Decision).

119/ 1923 P.C.I.J. (ser. A) No. 1.

120/ 1951 I.C.J. 71.

intervention in the case submitted by Libya and Tunisia,[121] and in 1984 Italy was denied intervention in the dispute submitted by Libya and Malta.[122] Later in 1984, the Court denied El Salvador's petition under Article 63 to intervene in the *Nicaragua*. In none of these three cases did the Court provide a clear explanation of its reasons for denying intervention. A central factor in the ICJ's decisions in the *Continental Shelf* cases, which were brought pursuant to a special agreement between the parties, undoubtedly was the opposition by both parties to intervention. Parties entering into special agreements generally may frame the scope of the case, both as to the parties and the subject matter to be resolved, as they agree. The Court may have been reluctant to interfere with this right.[123] Nevertheless, Nicaragua was permitted limited intervention in *Land, Island & Maritime Frontier Dispute*.

The ICJ's Rules (Article 81) require states seeking to intervene under Article 62 to specify any basis for jurisdiction that might exist between it and the parties to the case. In *Land, Island & Maritime Frontier Dispute*, the Court expressly rejected the argument that there must be a jurisdictional link between the prospective intervenor and the parties, but whether there is a jurisdictional may be considered by the Court. It is somewhat inconsistent with the Court's jurisdictional limitations to permit a state to intervene in a proceeding if that state could not directly initiate a case against the parties. The ICJ explained, however, that intervenors do not become full parties to the case and that the scope of their participation is limited to the extent necessary to protect their interests.

On the other hand, to permit litigation that might affect a third state without allowing that state to participate in the case offends fundamental notions of justice. In the *Libya-Malta Continental Shelf* case, the ICJ went to great lengths to avoid prejudicing Italy's interests. Instead of drawing a boundary line between Libya and Malta over the entire area in dispute, the Court truncated the line at the earliest point where Italy would arguably have an interest. In effect, this gave Italy everything it might have obtained if it had been permitted to intervene. Judge Schwebel, who would have allowed intervention, dissented from limiting the boundary line. He would have drawn the line as requested by the parties over the entire area in dispute, but would have indicated that the Court was not taking any position on where the boundary with Italy intersected that line. This was the approach taken in the *Libya-Tunisia Continental Shelf* case.

Judge Schwebel was certainly correct. No purpose was served by truncating the boundary line, since Italy was not bound by the decision. Indeed, even if Italy had participated in the case, other states might have claims to the area in question. The *Continental Shelf* cases do not foreclose another state from, for example, asserting that that portion of the continental shelf lies outside the jurisdiction of any state.[124] By truncating the line, the Court did not fully resolve the issue submitted to it by Libya and Malta. If states believe that the

---

121/ *Continental Shelf (Tunesia v. Libya)*, 1981 I.C.J. 3 (Intervention).

122/ *Continental Shelf (Malta v. Libya)*, 1984 I.C.J. 3 (Intervention).

123/ A similar argument can be made with cases having other jurisdictional bases. Parties to compromissory clauses have agreed to Court jurisdiction only over disputes with other parties to the treaty at issue, and states submitting declarations under the optional clause have also agreed only to be to parties to cases with other states submitting declarations.

124/ Essentially all the Court can say in any maritime boundary case is, for example, that Malta has no claim to territory on the Libyan side of the line and Libya has no claim to territory on the Maltese side of the line.

Court will not completely resolve their dispute they may avoid the ICJ and seek some other method of resolution.

The Court's refusal to grant intervention in the *Continental Shelf* cases was shortsighted. It is difficult to envision how the interests of the parties would have been adversely affected by allowing intervention. Intervention would have demonstrated that the Court is open to hearing the views of all potentially affected parties, and it would have allowed the efficient resolution of the boundary disputes concerning the Mediterranean continental shelf. For example, the second case between Libya and Malta might not have been necessary if Malta had been permitted to intervene in the case between Libya and Tunisia. Nonetheless, there was no real harm in denying intervention in these cases as the states seeking intervention were not prejudiced by the decisions.

This was not the case with respect to denial of El Salvador's declaration of intervention in the *Nicaragua* proceeding. Nicaragua based its claim in part on provisions of multilateral conventions, including the Charters of the U.N. and the OAS. El Salvador, a party to these Charters, sought to intervene pursuant to Article 63 "for the sole and limited purpose of arguing that this Court does not have jurisdiction over Nicaragua's Application . . . and that such Application and claims are inadmissible."[125] The Court denied intervention, apparently because it viewed the El Salvador's petition as primarily directed to the merits of the case and not to the preliminary matters of jurisdiction and admissibility. The ICJ indicated, however, that El Salvador could petition to intervene in the merits phase of the proceeding.

The most disturbing aspect of the Court's action was its failure to grant El Salvador a hearing on its request. The Court's rules require that a hearing be granted if any party objects to an intervention request. Although Nicaragua did not formally object to El Salvador's declaration, it did point out what it called "deficiencies" in the petition. The Court found that El Salvador was not under these circumstances entitled to a hearing on its request. Denial of a hearing on El Salvador's intervention declaration needlessly harmed the credibility of the Court and was cited by the U.S. as evidence of the Court's bias. The ICJ should reasonably have construed Nicaragua's submission pointing out "deficiencies" in the declaration as an objection that would require that hearing. Moreover, even if not required by its Rules, the Court certainly had discretion to hold a hearing—discretion it should have exercised. Besides giving the appearance of fairness, a hearing might have elicited information or arguments that would have improved the Court's decisionmaking.

One of the principal justifications given by the Court for denying interventions is that under Article 59 its judgments are binding only upon the parties to the dispute before it and only with respect to that dispute. Thus, the Court reasons that because a judgment does not bind a third-party, the third-party cannot by prejudiced by the judgment since it can raise the matter anew in a subsequent proceeding. This provides inadequate protection to would-be intervenors. While the Court is not required to follow its past decisions, as a practical matter,

---

125/ Declaration of Intervention of the Republic of El Salvador (Aug. 15, 1984), *reprinted in* 24 I.L.M. 38 (1985). While not the model of clarity, El Salvador's declaration in *Nicaragua* seemed to be limited to the preliminary phase of the proceeding. El Salvador appears to have wanted to argue that the case should not proceed because it was an indispensable party and there was no jurisdictional basis upon which Nicaragua could bring it into the case. It may have wanted to limit its participation to the preliminary phase as a means of avoiding being bound by the judgment on the merits. Such a position is disingenuous. If El Salvador was going to intervene, it should have intended to participate fully in those portions of the case in which it had an interest, and it should have expected to be bound by the judgment.

it does rely upon them in future cases. Once the ICJ rules on an issue in the initial proceeding, it will be extremely difficult for a third-party state to convince the Court to modify its reasoning in a subsequent proceeding involving the same dispute.[126] While in some proceedings, such as the *Continental Shelf* cases, the fact that a third state is not bound by the judgment will be adequate protection for its rights. This was not the case in *Nicaragua*. A central issue in that proceeding was whether U.S. actions against Nicaragua were justified as collective self-defense in support of El Salvador. An order preventing the U.S. from assisting El Salvador clearly would affect that country. While the Court seemed to feel that El Salvador's declaration related to the merits of the case rather than the preliminary phase, this appears to be incorrect. El Salvador specifically asked to address admissibility and had a legitimate interest in these issues.[127] Consequently, there was no good reason for disallowing intervention with respect to admissibility, especially since no party formally objected.[128]

The ICJ's reluctance to allow intervention is unfortunate and if continued could harm its credibility and effectiveness. Reasonable intervention is both fair and expedient. Recent decisions of the ICJ indicate that it may be relaxing its resistance to intervention.

The distinction between Article 62 and Article 63 interventions should be abandoned. Two types of intervention should be allowed. States with an actual interest in a proceeding should be permitted to intervene unless there is a good reason to prohibit intervention. Unlike the Court's present practice, intervenors should be full parties to the proceeding and the judgment should be fully binding upon them. States that merely have an interest in how the Court address a legal issue, whether a question of customary international law or construction of a treaty (even if they are not a party to the treaty), could request the limited right to file comments on the legal issues. The Court should be as open as possible to such requests, but could limit them to avoid abuse or undue delay. Participation in this way should normally be limited to submission of written comments similar to *amicus curiae* briefs in U.S. courts, but the ICJ should have discretion to allow them greater participation. While an amendment to the Statute would be useful, some of these changes might be implemented by the Court through rulemaking.

126/ Of course, the Court's interpretation of international law might have relevance to future, unrelated disputes. Consequently even a state having no direct interest in the instant dispute, could have some interest in how the Court interprets international law in that dispute. The potential prejudice to a third-state under these circumstances is not as great, however, as it would be if the state had a direct interest in the present proceeding, since the Court could more easily distinguish a subsequent dispute on the merits in order to apply a different legal rule.

127/ There was little reason, however, to allow El Salvador to intervene with respect to jurisdiction. It had no basis whatsoever for commenting on the U.S.—Nicaragua FCN treaty and could add nothing to the U.S.'s arguments with respect to jurisdiction under the optional clause.

128/ El Salvador's attempted intervention under Article 63 was based upon it being a party to several conventions which Nicaragua cited in support of its legal arguments. However, because the Vandenberg reservation to the U.S.'s declaration limited jurisdiction in cases involving multilateral treaties, the Court expressly refrained from interpreting these conventions. Had the Court ruled at the preliminary stage of the proceeding that it would refrain from construing these conventions, intervention could have been denied for this reason. However, under such circumstances it would have been appropriate for the ICJ to have permitted El Salvador to resubmit its request under Article 62. Why El Salvador did not initially submit its request under both provisions is a mystery.

B. Indispensable Parties

In a few instances the Court has considered whether the fair, and complete resolution of a case required the participation of absent states. Concerns raised in such cases include possible prejudice to the parties or the absent states and the possibility that only the absent states could provide the factual information necessary to resolve the case. In domestic situations, where the court has jurisdiction over an essential party, the solution to the indispensable party problem is to join the party to the case. Compelled participation by a third state in a proceeding before the World Court, however, is not currently possible unless there is a basis for jurisdiction over the state. The solution to indispensable party situations at the international level may, if the judgment cannot be limited to avoid prejudicing any state, be dismissal of the case. As a result, the Court has been reluctant to find that an absent state is indispensable to the just resolution of a proceeding.

The first case involving an indispensable party was an advisory opinion of the PCIJ in *Status of Eastern Carelia.*[129] When the Soviet Union refused a request of Finland to adjudicate the status of a territory between the two countries, the League of Nations sought an advisory opinion. The PCIJ declined to rule on the case in part because of the difficulty of deciding factual issues without the participation of a directly interested party. *Monetary Gold*[130] was an outgrowth of the *Corfu Channel* case,[131] in which Albania was found liable to the U.K. for damages resulting from the mining of the Corfu Channel. Albania did not pay the judgment. *Monetary Gold* involved gold that had been removed from Italy during the war and was in the custody of a commission composed of the U.S., the U.K. and France that was ruling on claims to the gold. An arbitrator ruled that the gold belonged to Albania. The commission, however, agreed that the gold would be handed over to the U.K. in partial satisfaction of the *Corfu Channel* judgment unless either Italy or Albania instituted proceedings against them in the ICJ. Italy instituted suit, but argued that the Court could not resolve the matter without the participation of Albania. The Court agreed. It found that Albania's interests were the very subject matter of the case. This was certainly correct. There was no real dispute between Italy and the members of the commission—the dispute was between Albania and the U.K. The commission's action was a subterfuge designed to force Albania to submit the case to the Court's jurisdiction. The Court quite reasonably would not be a party to this subterfuge.

The question of indispensable parties arose again in *Nicaragua*. The U.S. viewed the matter as a regional dispute that could not be fairly resolved without the participation of other states in the region, especially Honduras which Nicaragua alleged was used as a staging ground for the unlawful activities directed toward it. The U.S. argued that the case would affect the rights of other states, that the Court cannot decide the rights of absent states without their consent or participation, and that absent states possessed factual information relevant to the proceeding.

The ICJ unanimously rejected the U.S. position on indispensable parties. After noting that only the parties will be bound by the judgment, the Court stated:

129/ P.C.I.J., ser. B, No. 5 (1923).

130/ 1954 I.C.J. 19.

131/ 1949 I.C.J. 4, 244.

> [O]ther States which consider that they may be affected are free to institute separate proceedings, or to employ the procedure of intervention. There is no trace, either in the Statute or in the practice of international tribunals, of an "indispensable parties" rule of the kind argued by the United States, which only would be conceivable in parallel to a power, which the Court does not possess, to direct that a third State be made a party to proceedings. The circumstances of the *Monetary Gold* case probably represent the limit of the power of the Court to refuse to exercise its jurisdiction.[132]

The court was certainly correct. There are instances in which dismissal of a case will be appropriate. The *Monetary Gold* situation where the entire case revolves around the absent state's interests is one. Cases where the respondent state will be significantly prejudiced may be another. For example, the Court probably should not decide a case where the respondent cannot obtain essential evidence, whether because of an absent state or some other reason. Potential prejudice to the absent state is a much less compelling reason for dismissal. What is important is that potentially interested states be afforded an opportunity to participate in the proceeding. There is no unfairness if states have an effective right to intervene, irrespective of whether they elect to exercise that right. The principle that submission to ICJ jurisdiction is voluntary is not violated by requiring a state to choose between intervention, where it can present its position and be bound by the judgment, and nonintervention, where it may be indirectly affected by the judgment. It would go too far to allow a third state with an interest in the dispute to block a case otherwise properly before the court merely because it declines to participate. That would reward nonparticipation. Of course, the Court should avoid anything in its judgment that needlessly affects an absent state, and should ensure that interested states do have a real and effective right to intervene.

132/ 1984 I.C.J. 392, 431, *reprinted in* 24 I.L.M. 59, 78 (1985). *Certain Phosphate Lands in Nauru (Nauru v. Australia)*, 1992 I.C.J. 240, concerned the administration of Nauru by Australia, New Zealand, and the U.K. first as a Mandate of the League of Nations and then as a Trusteeship under the U.N. Nauru brought this proceeding against Australia for environmental damage that had resulted from the actions by the three administering states in mining rich phosphate deposits on the island. Although all three states were the administering authority under the trusteeship agreement, Australia had in fact administered Nauru on behalf of all three nations. The Court rejected Australia's claim that New Zealand and the U.K. were indispensable parties. The ICJ noted that unlike *Monetary Gold* the interests of the absent states did not form the very subject-matter of the case and that a finding on Australia's liability did not depend on a finding concerning the liability of the absent parties.

X. Proof of Facts

While some cases involve no disputed facts and turn solely upon the Court's interpretation of the law, others present the Court with substantial factual issues. Most factual issues are resolved through the pleadings, documentary evidence attached to the pleadings, and oral argument. Relatively few cases have presented the testimony of live witnesses, including expert witnesses. A number of cases, including *Nicaragua* and several maritime boundary cases, have presented the Court with extensive factual questions.[133]

The Statute does not deal with the Court's power over factual issues in detail, providing only a general framework. It gives the Court authority to make orders for the conduct of the case, call upon the parties to produce documents or provide explanations, and make rules of procedure governing the taking of evidence. The Statute also authorizes the Court to appoint an individual or body to carry out an enquiry or give an expert opinion.[134] In some types of cases, such as boundary disputes, there is little difficulty in obtaining the relevant evidence. The parties generally present detailed maps and expert testimony by, e.g., geologists, in support of their positions. Other cases present particular evidentiary problems. Where, as in *Nicaragua* there is an ongoing conflict, determining the relevant facts may be particularly difficult.[135] States may be especially reluctant, for example, to disclose to the Court evidence obtained from intelligence sources, because of the danger it would present to their intelligence operations. The U.S. decision to not defend the *Nicaragua* case may have been prompted in part by the fact that much of the evidence in support of the U.S. position came from such sources.

In *Nicaragua* and earlier in *Corfu Channel*, the ICJ described some of the rules it would apply in evaluating the weight to be given different kinds of evidence. The ICJ has developed a best evidence rule for documentary evidence[136] and has noted that hearsay is often of little value.[137] In *Nicaragua* the Court struggled with the value to be given to public statements by public officials. The ICJ found that such statements were of high evidentiary value when they acknowledge facts that are unfavorable to their state, but were of little value when they were self-serving. This rule concerning admissions against a party's interest is comparable to the rule followed in U.S. courts. The case also dealt with the weight to be given to reports

---

133/ *See generally* K. Highet, *Evidence and Proof of Facts*, in Crossroads, *supra* note 23, at 355.

134/ Little use has been made of this provision. In *Corfu Channel*, the Court did appoint a committee of experts to evaluate complex evidence, and obtained the opinion of two additional experts as to the amount of damages.

135/ The Court noted that "One of the Court's chief difficulties in the present case has been the determination of the facts relevant to the dispute." It also noted that in view of the continuing nature of the conflict, the judgment would be based upon events occurring up to the close of oral argument. 1986 I.C.J. 39—39.

136/ The rule generally requires that the actual original document be produced, rather than, e.g., a copy or summary, unless it can be shown that the original is unavailable.

137/ "The statements attributed by the witness Kovacic to third parties, of which the Court has received no personal and direct conformation, can be regarded only as allegations falling short of conclusive evidence." *Corfu Channel,* 1949 I.C.J. at 16—17.

in the press. The Court generally accepted as public knowledge information that was widely reported in the press, especially press reports that were not denied by the responsible state or which reported on official statements of responsible officials. The Court was careful to disregard testimony which was a statement of opinion rather than a statement of fact. Judge Schwebel criticized some of these evidentiary rulings.[138] For example, the ruling concerning admissions by public officials may place democracies and other open societies at a disadvantage. While to a certain extent, some of these criticisms may be valid, the Court probably did as well as it could in view of the failure of the U.S. to participate in the proceeding.

A. The Problem of Non-Appearance

The Court's factual determinations can only be as reliable as the evidence upon which they are based.[139] The weakest link in the ICJ's decisionmaking process is its inability to compel states to produce relevant evidence. While the Court may draw inferences from a party's failure to produce evidence, it has no way to encourage non-parties to provide evidence. Obtaining necessary evidence is particularly difficult where the respondent state refuses to participate in the proceeding.

Even though the Court has jurisdiction, respondent states are not required to participate actively in the proceedings, and oftentimes they do not. The fact that many respondents have failed to appear is symptomatic of the lack of respect that many states have for the Court.[140] Failure to appear does not result in a default judgment for the applicant. Article 53 of the Statute provides that before it can rule for the applicant, the ICJ must satisfy itself that it has jurisdiction and that "the claim is well founded in fact and law." In *Nicaragua* the ICJ noted that "in a case of nonappearance, neither party should be placed at a disadvantage; therefore the party which declines to appear cannot be permitted to profit from its absence."[141] By

---

138/ 1986 I.C.J. at 321—31.

139/ In his dissent, Judge Schwebel would have held the critical issue of whether the U.S. claim of self-defense was justified to be nonjusticiable because of the insurmountable evidentiary problems the case presented. He maintained that it was not possible for the Court to reach a confident judgment on the policies and motives of the states concerned, given the absence of the U.S. and other states involved in the Central American conflict and the unwillingness, in part based upon security considerations, of the states concerned to provide necessary evidence. 1986 I.C.J. at 294—95.

140/ *See generally* J. Charney, *Disputes Implicating the Institutional Credibility of the Court*, in CROSSROADS, *supra* note 23, at 288. Respondents have failed to appear in *Trial of Pakistani Prisoners of War (Pak. v. India), Fisheries Jurisdiction (U.K. & Ger. v. Ice.), Nuclear Test Cases (Austl. & N.Z. v. Fr.), Aegean Sea Continental Shelf (Greece v. Turk.),* and the *Hostages* Case. In some proceedings, states have appeared in one stage but not in another. In *Corfu Channel*, Albania appeared in the merits phase, but not in the compensation phase. Iran appeared in the jurisdiction but not the preliminary measures phase of *Anglo-Iranian Oil Company (U.K. v. Iran).* Guatemala did not appear in the jurisdiction phase but did appear in the subsequent phase of the *Nottebohm Case (Guat. v. Lict.).* Finally, in *Nicaragua* the U.S. appeared at the interim measures and preliminary objections phase but not in the merits or compensation phase.

141/ 1986 I.C.J. at 26. In his dissent, Judge Schwebel argued that if the non-appearing party raises an affirmative defense, e.g. self-defense, the appearing party must demonstrate that it is not valid in order to (Cont'd)

declining to appear, a state gives up the right to submit evidence and argument in support of its position, and the right to counter or cross examine the appearing state's evidence and witnesses. The Court may attempt to equalize the position of the parties by, for example, itself subjecting the appearing state's witnesses to cross examination. In addition, the Court may receive informal communications from the absent state or, as was the case in *Nicaragua*, it may have the benefit of the state's submissions in a prior phase of the case. Such measures cannot fully substitute for full participation in a case, however. The Court cannot be expected to anticipate all issues that the absent party might raise or ask witnesses all the questions that a party might ask. It was unfortunate that the U.S. did not defend the *Nicaragua* case. The U.S. might have obtained a more favorable result had it mounted a vigorous defense.

B. Improving the Method of Proving Facts

In any event, the ICJ should better utilize the evidentiary powers it does have. It might make greater use of its authority to appoint expert witnesses and commissions of enquiry to help it investigate and evaluate difficult factual issues.[142] A commission of enquiry could, for example, assist in situations where a state has relevant intelligence information that it does not wish to become public. A commission of persons acceptable to both parties could be appointed to receive such evidence *in camera* under the condition that it would not reveal anything that the submitter of the evidence considered sensitive. After evaluating the evidence the commission could issue a report to the Court giving its conclusions on what the evidence demonstrates. While this would not give the opposing state the ability to directly examine the evidence, it could provide a reasonable compromise.

Enhancement of the Court's authority to obtain evidence is needed. Many states have entered into judicial assistance treaties that allow them to request another state to assist it in obtaining evidence for use in proceedings in its courts. Such treaties include provisions for the taking of depositions and the production of documents. These treaties give domestic courts greater rights to obtain evidence from another state than is possessed by the ICJ. The

141/ (Cont'd)
prevail. *Id.* at 320. This would shift the burden of showing the affirmative defense from the non-appearing to the appearing party. This would go too far, since it would reward non-participation. Certainly, it should be sufficient that the appearing state show that there is substantial doubt as to the validity of the affirmative defense, but it should not be required to prove that the defense is not valid.

142/ Judge Schwebel criticized the Court in his dissent in *Nicaragua* for not conducting an adequate investigation into the facts of the case:

> [I]t might have been thought that the Court would have chosen to make use of those considerable powers in obtaining evidence . . . . It could, for example, . . . have entrusted an appropriate commission of judges or another organization with the task of carrying out a fact-finding enquiry in the territories of Nicaragua, the United States, El Salvador, Honduras, Costa Rica, Guatemala and Cuba . . . .
>
> Quite without justification, it even failed to request El Salvador to transmit the "positive proof" of Nicaraguan subversion that it claimed to possess [in its request to intervene]. The Court goes so far as to hold that there is no evidence that El Salvador ever requested . . . that the United States give it assistance in collective self-defence. But it failed to invite El Salvador to transmit evidence in support of its official claim to the Court that it had made such requests . . . .

1986 I.C.J. at 322—23

Court should have at least as much evidence gathering capability as is typically provided by judicial assistance treaties. The Statute should be amended to give the Court greater powers to compel the production of evidence. Alternatively, states should enter into a convention patterned after judicial assistance treaties.

ICJ proceedings would be improved if the Court exercised greater control over the presentation of evidence. The Court has permitted parties to submit virtually whatever evidence they believe appropriate. The submissions of some parties often give little indication of what the evidence submitted is intended to prove. This has led upon occasion to very lengthy submissions, often containing material that the Court eventually finds irrelevant to its decision in the case. While the Court has exercised greater control over recent cases, its Rules and procedures should be improved to better cope with factual disputes. Better guidance on the form of evidentiary submissions is necessary.[143] The parties should be required to clarify in greater detail what their evidence is intended to prove, and the Court should limit the introduction of evidence that it finds irrelevant or repetitious. Prehearing conferences (before either the President or a panel of several judges) could be conducted for the purpose of clarifying the parties' positions and narrowing the factual issues to be resolved. Such prehearing conferences could, for example, obtain admissions from the parties concerning facts they do not dispute, thereby eliminating the need to produce evidence on those issues. Besides helping the Court to understand the parties' positions and evidentiary submissions, conferences could provide the parties with some indication of the issues that the Court believes are important. A conference could be followed by orders concerning what and how evidence concerning various matters will be presented. Such improvements would expedite the oral proceedings and make them more valuable to the Court.

143/ Some commentators have suggested that there be limits on the length of evidentiary submissions. This would be difficult to apply in practice since some disputes are more complex than others and would necessarily require more detailed and lengthy submissions.

XI. Ensuring Compliance with ICJ Judgments

Obtaining a favorable decision from the Court may be a hollow victory if the losing side does not comply with the judgment. Effective means exist to secure compliance with judgments of domestic courts in disputes between private individuals. If the losing side of a domestic case does not comply, the prevailing party may return to the court for assistance. The court may, for example, direct the sheriff to seize and sell property of the defendant to satisfy a money judgment, or it may direct the sheriff to arrest the defendant and bring him before the court which can impose sanctions, such as imprisonment, to coerce compliance with an injunction or other court order. As a result, in most domestic cases, the losing party will comply with the judgment or will negotiate a settlement that both parties can accept.

A similar model was contemplated for the World Court. The Statute provides that states are bound to comply with the Court's judgments,[144] and the drafters of the Court's Statute expected nations to comply as a matter of course. There is significant international pressure to comply, since most states want to be viewed as upholding the rule of law not as international outlaws. Article 94(2) of the U.N. Charter further provides that if a party fails to comply with a judgment, "the other party may have recourse to the Security Council which may, if it deems necessary, make recommendations or decide upon measures to be taken to give effect to the judgment."

Compliance with arbitral awards and judgments of the PCIJ was remarkably good. Similarly, there has been a good record of compliance with ICJ judgments in proceedings initiated by special agreements. In cases where jurisdiction was based on a compromissory clause or the optional clause, compliance with ICJ judgments has been disappointing, and in the case of provisional measures, noncompliance has been the rule.[145] In some cases where a state has rejected an ICJ judgment it has nonetheless negotiated a settlement of the case, often in conjunction with a settlement of a larger dispute. For example, Iran did not participate in the *Hostages* case and took no steps to comply with the judgment. However, the dispute concerning the hostages was resolved as part of a settlement that dealt with a number of other issues, including Iran's claims to frozen assets and to payments due it for goods received. Under such circumstances, an ICJ judgment can be expected to play a significant, but not controlling, role in the negotiations. In several cases, however, states have ignored Court judgments completely. The 1954 judgment in *Corfu Channel* remains unsatisfied, and the U.S. took no steps to comply with the *Nicaragua* judgment. That case was

---

144/ This is only true in contentious cases. Advisory opinions are by their nature not binding and they cannot be enforced. Nevertheless, advisory opinions carry considerable weight and states often follow them, even when it is not necessarily in their self-interest to do so. Certainly, U.N. bodies adhere to international law as reflected in ICJ advisory opinions, since ignoring the rule of law can have dangerous consequences. Unfortunately, the U.N. itself has ignored advisory opinions on several occasions.

145/ *See* J. Charney, *Disputes Implicating the Institutional Credibility of the Court,* CROSSROADS, *supra* note 23, 288. Enforcement of the judgment is seldom an issue when the Court rules for the defendant. The plaintiff state usually stops asserting the claim.

settled only because the new Nicaraguan government decided to drop it in order to maintain good relations with the U.S and to obtain U.S. financial aid.[146]

A. Security Council Enforcement

The Security Council has been unable to fulfill the role of sheriff that was contemplated by the Statute. Whether to take action to enforce a judgment is a matter within the Council's discretion.[147] Under its Statute, ICJ decisions are final; consequently, the Council should not in theory reexamine them. As with other matters, however, the Council in exercising its discretion is not bound by international law, and it may ignore an ICJ judgment or impose a different solution where it finds that it will diminish a threat to peace.

Until the last few years, the divisions in the Council caused by Cold War made it likely that some permanent member would veto any constructive action to enforce an ICJ judgment.[148] Now that the end of the Cold War has increased cooperation in the Security Council, there is a greater possibility that it will be able to play the role of sheriff as intended by the Charter. Of course, there is virtually no chance that the Council will enforce a judgment against a permanent member or any judgment with which a permanent member strongly disagrees.[149]

There are several actions the Council can take to encourage compliance with a judgment. First, it can call on the recalcitrant state to comply with the judgment and it may suggest methods by which it can satisfy this obligation that might be acceptable to both parties. In addition, the agreements between most specialized agencies and the U.N require the agencies

---

146/ Since Nicaragua did not drop the suit until economic assistance was assured, some have viewed this in effect as a "*quid pro quo*" settlement.

147/ The Security Council's role is patterned after the enforcement role of the Council of the League of Nations. There are differences however. The League Covenant gave the Council authority to enforce awards of other international tribunals as well as those of the PCIJ, and it required the Council to take steps to enforce any judicial decision. In 1933 Greece received an award in the *Rhodopia Forest* case. Bulgaria was unwilling to pay the judgment until the matter was placed on the League Council's agenda. It then promptly agreed to comply. The League Council had more difficulties with *Optant's Case*, when Hungary sought to force Rumania to comply with the judgment. The Council was sympathetic toward Rumania's position, and created a commission to study the matter. The commission decided on a different result and effectively nullified the award. *See generally* O'Connell, *supra* note 111, at 906—07.

148/ The Council voted overwhelmingly to call on the U.S. to comply with the *Nicaragua* judgment, but the U.S. vetoed the resolution. The U.K. asked the Council to enforce an order indicating provisional measures in *Anglo-Iranian Oil Co. (U.K. v. Iran)*, 1951 I.C.J. 4 (Interim Protection Order of July 5). The Soviet Union and Yugoslavia opposed the request, asserting that the dispute was a matter of Iran's domestic jurisdiction and that the Council could not act until the ICJ found it had jurisdiction. The request became moot before the Council acted on the request.

149/ There is some question as to whether the veto applies to requests to enforcement judgments. *See generally* O'Connell, *supra* note 111, at 908. Some commentators have suggested that the veto should not apply to enforcement of Court decisions because Article 94 is not located in the Chapters dealing with peace and security which contain the veto. On the other hand, Article 27(3) of the Charter specifies that in issues before the Council under Chapter VI, any party to a dispute shall not vote. But, Council practice has been to allow permanent members to use the veto even in Chapter VI disputes to which they are a party.

to assist the Security Council in the maintenance of international peace and security.[150] The Council could direct these agencies to turn over assets of the judgment debtor or impose sanctions such as withholding benefits. Finally, the Council could enlist the assistance of member states. It could call on them, and perhaps order them, to take steps to encourage compliance.[151] If, for example, in a case involving a boundary dispute the losing party refused to withdraw to the border recognized in the judgment, the Council could require all members to refuse to recognize the recalcitrant state's occupation of the territory. In other cases, the Security Council might impose a mandatory trade embargo or direct a third state to seize assets of the judgment debtor and turn them over to the creditor in partial satisfaction of the judgment.

B. Enforcement Through Domestic Courts

The judgment creditor, or an individual or firm on whose behalf it espoused the claim, might seek enforcement of a money judgment through its own courts or through the courts of a third-party state.[152] Not all governmental assets may be seized to satisfy a judgment. Generally, property used for traditional governmental purposes, such a embassies, embassy bank accounts, and warships, cannot be attached, while property used for "commercial" purposes, such as research vessels and material at trade shows, can be attached. The ability to attach a debtor state's assets and the procedures it must follow will depend upon the domestic law of the state through whose courts enforcement is sought. A few states adhere to the monist theory of international law. Under this theory, international law is considered part, and usually a superior part, of the domestic law of the state. A state following the monist theory would likely afford an ICJ judgment at least as much authority as it would a judgment of one of its domestic courts. Enforcement of a judgment in such a state would be through the same procedures as any domestic court judgment. Most states, however, are not part of the monist school, and enforcement of judgments in such states may be difficult. *Socobelge v. Greece*[153], one of the few cases to attempt enforcement in a domestic court, is illustrative.

150/ *See* O'Connell, *supra* note 111, at 910—12. A number of agencies may on their own initiative take action to enforce ICJ judgments related to matters within the agency's scope of authority. For example, the ILO Constitution provides in Article 33 that if a member fails to comply with an ICJ judgment, the "Governing Body may recommend to the Conference such action as it may deem wise and expedient to secure compliance therewith."

151/ The extent to which the Council can require states to implement sanctions where there is no threat to peace is debatable. Some states and commentators have contended that the Council cannot require third states to impose sanctions where there is no threat to peace. Others have contended that the Council has no authority to take any action to enforce judgments that do not relate to threats to peace. There does not seem to be any basis for either restriction. Article 94 is not contained in the Chapters relating to peace and security and nothing in its language implies any limitations on Council authority to enforce judgments. If enforcement of judgments were so limited, it would make Article 94 superfluous since the Charter already gives the Council authority over matters that threaten peace.

152/ Following the order for provisional measures issued in *Anglo-Iranian Oil Co. (U.K. v. Iran)*, 1951 I.C.J. 4 (Interim Protection Order of July 5), the oil company on whose behalf the claim was espoused succeeded in having the order enforced in a court in Aden.

153/ 1951 I.L.R. 3.

Belgium obtained a PCIJ judgment against Greece on a claim it espoused on behalf of Socobelge. The firm sought to enforce the judgment in Belgian courts by attaching Greek assets in that country. The court treated the claim the same as a judgment of a foreign country. Because Socobelge had not first obtained an *exequatur*, as required by Belgian law, the court declined to enforce the judgment. Many nations require an *exequatur*, which is a court order giving a foreign judgment the same force as a judgment of a domestic court, before they will enforce a foreign judgment. Procedures vary, but most states reexamine to some extent the merits of the case before granting an *exequatur.* However, review by domestic courts of ICJ judgements is inconsistent with the Statute's provision that judgments are final. Moreover, ICJ decisions should be entitled to more favorable treatment than judgments of a foreign state. A domestic court should not, for example, review the merits of an ICJ judgment before deciding whether to enforce it.

> The way to comprehensive security lies through strengthening the legal basis of international life, laid down primarily by the U.N. Charter, and through enhancing the role of the Organization which, in fact, represents a mechanism for translating the idea of the primacy of international law into reality. . . . Making law effective requires painstaking work by all states. Of special importance is whether individual states respect the priority of international law in foreign policy as well as internal legislation, whether they are guided by law in practice. It is necessary to overcome legal nihilism. Law should not be perceived as ancillary to politics.
>
> *Soviet U.N. Official V.F Petrovsky*
> *Report to the U.N. (October, 1988)*

Enforcement of a judgment in the courts of the losing state may also be possible. Certainly, if the executive branch of the government is resisting the judgment, recourse to the courts of the debtor state will only succeed if the state has a strong, independent judiciary that is committed to the rule of law. Even then, enforcement may be difficult. Following the *Nicaragua* judgment, a group of organizations and of U.S. citizens living in Nicaragua sued to enforce the judgment's order prohibiting the government from further support of the Contras.[154] The case was dismissed primarily on two grounds. First, the court found that only Nicaragua, not the plaintiffs, who were citizens of the U.S., had standing to seek enforcement of the ICJ judgment. Second, the court noted that the U.S. is a dualist, not a monist, state. While international law governs the relationships among states, as applied within the U.S. it is on a par with, not superior to, domestic law. Consequently, international law could be nullified, insofar as U.S. courts are concerned, by a subsequent, inconsistent Congressional statute. The court found that by appropriating funds to support the Contras, Congress had implicitly repealed for U.S. purposes, the international law applied in the *Nicaragua* judgment. The court concluded that it could not direct the U.S. to cease supporting the Contras. Had Nicaragua sued to enforce a monetary judgment, the result might have been different. Nicaragua would have had standing and a monetary judgment probably

154/ *Committee of U.S. Citizens Living in Nicaragua v. Reagan*, 859 F.2d 929 (D.C. Cir. 1988). The political question doctrine may also, under some circumstances, bar proceedings in U.S. courts. This doctrine is based upon the concept of separation of powers, and it requires courts to refrain from ruling on issues committed to another branch of government, such as the conduct of foreign policy. Although, the district court dismissed this case on political question grounds, the court of appeals found that it did not apply in this case.

would not have been deemed repealed unless Congress passed a law specifically prohibiting enforcement of the judgment.

C. Other Enforcement Mechanisms

The aggrieved state might also utilize various self-help measures to secure compliance. Such measures include seizing or freezing assets, imposing economic or trade sanctions, and limiting rights such as fishing, docking, landing or overflight rights. The right to engage in self-help is not unlimited. It will be governed by both international law and the state's domestic law. Under international law, the steps taken must not be disproportionate to the injury sustained, and they should not be such as to escalate the conflict or present the possibility that it will lead to a breach of the peace.

Assistance might also be sought from regional organizations[155] or from states unrelated to the ICJ proceeding. In many cases, third-party states may be reluctant to become embroiled in the dispute. In some, however, a third-party state might be willing to provide assistance.[156]

More effective means are needed to ensure enforcement of ICJ judgments. The credibility of the Court suffers when its judgments are ignored and cannot be enforced. Moreover, states will be reluctant to undergo the expense of litigation if there is little hope of enforcing a favorable judgment.[157] If the Court is to play its intended role in world affairs, it is essential that its decisions have meaning. The Security Council should be willing to enforce judgments even if some of its members disagree with those judgments. Nations, including the U.S., should amend their domestic laws to make it easier to enforce ICJ judgments in their courts. The Convention on the Recognition and Enforcement of Foreign Arbitral Awards[158] requires states to enforce arbitral awards as if they were decisions of their own courts. As a result, it is easier to enforce arbitral awards than ICJ judgments.[159] At a minimum, ICJ judgments should be treated as favorably as arbitral awards. Either the convention should be expanded to include ICJ judgments, or there should be a new convention dealing with enforcement of ICJ judgments.

155/ For example, the American Treaty on Pacific Settlement (Pact of Bogota), April 30, 1948, 30 U.N.T.S. 55, provides in Article 50 that before resorting to the Security Council to enforce an ICJ or arbitral award, the party seeking enforcement shall "propose a Meeting of Consultation of Ministers of Foreign Affairs to agree upon appropriate measures to ensure fulfillment of the . . . award."

156/ The *Monetary Gold* case arose out of efforts by the Western Allies to cooperate in assisting enforcement of the *Corfu Channel* decision.

157/ Collecting on a judgment may not be the only motive for ICJ litigation. States may be more interested in the public airing of their grievances that ICJ litigation gives than whether they can enforce a judgment.

158/ The Convention is reprinted in 7 I.L.M. 1046 (1968) and is implemented in the U.S. by 9 U.S.C. §§ 201—08. The U.S. and many other nations have included reservations limiting it to cases involving commercial disputes.

159/ In *Minister of Defense of the Islamic Republic of Iran v. Gould*, 887 F.2d 1357 (9th Cir. 1989), the court held that Iran could enforce a decision of the Iran-U.S. Claims Tribunal against a U.S. corporation in U.S. courts.

XII. Conclusion & Summary of Recommendations

Adherence to the rule of law in relations among states would benefit all nations and people on our planet by increasing the prospect for world peace and justice. Where the rule of law is absent, either the rule of force prevails or anarchy reigns. The world community has made great strides during this century toward forging a world order that is based on law. The U.N., imperfect though it is, represents an enormous improvement over the previous world disorder. Nevertheless, improvements in the U.N. and the international legal system will be required if we are to attain the full benefits of the rule of law. The expectations of some that creation of the World Court would solve all problems of compliance with international law and would ensure peace were unrealistic. For example, neither the *Hostages* nor the *Nicaragua* cases resulted in compliance with international law or restoration of peace between the contending sides. But, the Court has been a modest success, and in the future it can play a much larger role in the fair and peaceful settlement of disputes.

All nations are not equal under the current world order. Many nations are privileged in that their power permits them to ignore international law with impunity. Establishing the rule of law in international affairs will demand the commitment of nations, especially the more powerful nations, to abide by the law even when they believe it is contrary to their immediate short-term interests. Law will give all nations, large and small alike, the opportunity to obtain just settlements of their disputes based upon their legal merits, rather than having settlements dictated by stronger nations as is often the case today. In return for setting an example by submitting to the rule of law, the stronger nations will help create a more just and peaceful world that will ultimately benefit all. States accepting the rule of law will gain a reputation for fair play and justice that carries with it both tangible and intangible benefits. The U.S. prides itself on its commitment to justice and fairness to other nations—it should demonstrate this commitment by embracing the rule of law.

The key to increased utilization of the ICJ is change in the attitude of states. States must appreciate that even though they may occasionally lose a case, in the long run everyone benefits from the rule of law. Rather than resisting the Court's jurisdiction, as the U.S. did in *Nicaragua*, nations should welcome adjudication as a means of resolving disputes. Nations must be confident, however, that the Court will fairly and effectively decide the cases before it. The ICJ can itself institute some changes to encourage use of the Court. The rule changes that it instituted in 1978 to make use of special chambers attractive to states is one example, but it should further clarify its rules to remove ambiguities concerning chamber practices. The Court should also make rule and policy changes to increase its evidence gathering capabilities, by, for example, greater use of commissions of enquiry. It should reexamine whether the assumptions it applied in *Nicaragua* concerning the weight to be given various types of evidence are appropriate. The Court should be more receptive to intervention requests, and should revise its rules to clarify the rights and obligations of intervening states. With respect to its advisory jurisdiction, the Court should continue to be receptive to expanding the types of cases that may be referred to it through screening committees, such as it does with appeals from UNAT. It should consider amendments to its rules to allow individuals whose interests are at stake in such cases to participate to a greater extent in the Court proceedings. In addition, changes in the Court's Statute to increase confidence in the Court might be considered such as changing the method of judicial elections, providing for life tenure, and increasing the Court's evidence gathering capabilities.

The rule of law would benefit most from an increase in the ICJ's jurisdiction to include allowing the U.N. and other international organizations to be parties to contentious cases and to provide for true compulsory jurisdiction for intra-state disputes. Permitting organizations to appear as parties in contentious cases would expedite the resolution of disputes concerning the organization and could prevent potential constitutional crises that might develop if a dispute arises concerning the scope of the organization's authority. Compulsory jurisdiction would promote fairness and equality among nations, both large and small, and is essential for the full realization of the rule of law. Only through compulsory jurisdiction would states, especially smaller states, be guaranteed that they can vindicate their rights through the judicial process. However, some on these changes would require amendment of the ICJ Statute which will be difficult to achieve. For example, there is at this time little support in the community of nations for true compulsory jurisdiction.

Nevertheless, there are a number of enhancements to the Court's jurisdiction that may be realizable in the short run. While amendments to the Statute to provide for these enhancements are desirable, many can be achieved, at least in part, through other means. International organizations should be encouraged to seek advisory opinions when there is a substantial dispute concerning a matter within the scope of their activities. To make it easier for them to obtain an advisory opinion, their constitutions could be amended to provide that only a specified minority of the members, e.g., 30 to 40 percent, are necessary to request an opinion. The General Assembly should authorize the Secretary General, as well as additional organizations, to request advisory opinions. Granting the Secretary General the authority to obtain advisory opinions should prove of considerable value to him in mediating the settlement of disputes. Consideration should also be given to amending the Statute so that all U.N. organs and agencies can obtain advisory opinions without first being authorized by the General Assembly and to permit certain types of non-governmental organizations, such as the International Committee of the Red Cross, to obtain advisory opinions. Finally, national courts should be permitted to obtain advisory opinions under some circumstances. Some of these enhancements can be accomplished by establishment by the General Assembly of a screening committee with authority to request advisory opinions on behalf of nation-states or organizations outside of the U.N. system. Such a committee might also give individuals and corporations limited access to the Court.

States can demonstrate their commitment to the rule of law by bringing disputes that are suitable to adjudication before the Court. They should signify their commitment by (1) including compromissory clauses in treaties (2) entering into a general dispute resolution convention that provides for ICJ resolution, and (3) accepting the Court's general jurisdiction under the optional clause. The U.S. should exercise leadership in this regard. It should, for example, emphasize its commitment to the rule of law by filing a new declaration under the optional clause that does not contain such debilitating reservations as the Connally reservation. Most importantly, where jurisdiction does exist, the U.S. should refer suitable disputes to the Court for resolution on a regular basis.

Treaties and compromissory clauses could, if the parties desire, allow for adjudication by special chambers, but to be effective such provisions must specify how that chamber will be selected. A broad general convention on dispute settlement, having uniform terms for all parties, may be a more desirable method of conferring jurisdiction than is the optional clause, where each state's declaration can be different.

This paper has focused primarily upon the role that the ICJ might play in establishing the rule of law. However, the rule of law also requires an equitable system of enacting laws and

> After a decade, the greater part of which was characterized by selfishness and arrogance, we need to restore global morality. We need the vision of being one global neighborhood. That is the idea of international solidarity, without which humankind might not survive the next century. We need a new world order, based on justice and peace, democracy and development, human rights and international law.
>
> *Common Responsibility in the 1990's: The Stockholm Initiative on Global Security & Governance (1991)*

an effective means of enforcing those laws. An equitable system of enacting international law will require some form of weighted voting system so that larger nations have a greater vote than smaller nations in the legislative body. To the extent that there is no effective method of international legislation, nations may be reluctant to resort to the ICJ because of the uncertainty in the law. They may also believe that a rule of customary international law is outdated and would be changed by the world community if there were a way to do so. Utilization of the ICJ also suffers from the lack of an effective method of enforcing judgments. If a state believes that the chance is small that a judgment will be complied with, it might well decide that adjudication is not worth the cost and effort. No nation should be above the law. The Security Council must place a greater priority on the enforcement of ICJ judgments. Furthermore, either the Statute should be amended or a convention, similar to the convention for enforcement of arbitral awards, should be drafted that would require states to enforce ICJ judgments. Even in the absence of such a requirement, however, nations, including the U.S., should amend their domestic laws to facilitate enforcement of ICJ judgments.

The outlook for a strengthened, more viable Court is bright provided the U.S. takes the initiative and receives the cooperation of most other major powers. The degree to which a nation supports the Court can, as with other things, change radically with a change in government. In the U.S., the Reagan and Bush administrations were not enthusiastic about ICJ adjudication. The Clinton administration, however, appears to be somewhat more receptive. Furthermore, until the breakup of the Soviet Union, President Gorbachev was taking steps to reverse the Soviet Union's historical hostility to judicial resolution of disputes.[160] Whether this trend will continue under Russian President Yeltsin, who appears preoccupied with domestic problems, is unclear. To a large degree, U.S. support for the Court will be dependant upon whether the American public supports the rule of law. Obtaining support of the public will require a change in the attitude of many citizens who believe that the U.S. can do no wrong and should never be subordinate to any international institution. The media should be enlisted to help educate the American people about the importance of world citizenship. The American public must recognize that we are all citizens of a world community and that the U.S. owes an obligation to obey the laws of that community in the same way that citizens have an obligation to obey domestic laws. The American public must understand that when all nations adhere to the rule of law, everyone will benefit from a more peaceful and ordered world.

160/ In March 1989, the Soviet Union reversed its previous position and accepted ICJ jurisdiction with respect to five human rights conventions. Later that year, the U.S. and the Soviet Union agreed to ICJ jurisdiction over disputes between them involving seven treaties to which they are parties. In September 1989, the Soviet Union called upon states to enter into a general dispute resolution treaty.